T0323599

Cambridge Elements ≡

Elements in the Gothic
edited by
Dale Townshend
Manchester Metropolitan University
Angela Wright
University of Sheffield

THE MUSIC OF THE GOTHIC 1789–1820

Emma McEvoy
University of Westminster

CAMBRIDGE
UNIVERSITY PRESS

Shaftesbury Road, Cambridge CB2 8EA, United Kingdom

One Liberty Plaza, 20th Floor, New York, NY 10006, USA

477 Williamstown Road, Port Melbourne, VIC 3207, Australia

314–321, 3rd Floor, Plot 3, Splendor Forum, Jasola District Centre,
New Delhi – 110025, India

103 Penang Road, #05–06/07, Visioncrest Commercial, Singapore 238467

Cambridge University Press is part of Cambridge University Press & Assessment,
a department of the University of Cambridge.

We share the University's mission to contribute to society through the pursuit of
education, learning and research at the highest international levels of excellence.

www.cambridge.org
Information on this title: www.cambridge.org/9781009532860

DOI: 10.1017/9781009170369

First published 2024

A catalogue record for this publication is available from the British Library

ISBN 978-1-009-53286-0 Hardback
ISBN 978-1-009-17037-6 Paperback
ISSN 2634-8721 (online)
ISSN 2634-8713 (print)

Additional resources for this publication at www.cambridge.org/McEvoy

The Music of the Gothic 1789–1820

Elements in the Gothic

DOI: 10.1017/9781009170369
First published online: December 2024

Emma McEvoy
University of Westminster

Author for correspondence: Emma McEvoy, E.McEvoy@westminster.ac.uk

Abstract: Music plays an essential role in Gothic between the years 1789 and 1820, but it signifies very differently at the end of the period compared with the beginning. In the 1790s, the music of Gothic novels and plays is not Gothic music as we conceive of it. It is celebratory, calming or transcendent rather than scary. By 1820, the music of Gothic is more likely to provoke shock, discomfort and unease. Melodrama brings about this change. Its ascendancy had long-lasting effects on the music of the Gothic more generally – in fiction and poetry, on the stage and the screen. The Element considers work by writers including Ann Radcliffe, Matthew Lewis, Eliza Fenwick, Samuel Taylor Coleridge and James Boaden in conjunction with music by composers such as Michael Kelly, Stephen Storace and Samuel Arnold. Audio files of the music accompany the Element.

This Element also has a video abstract: www.cambridge.org/ GOTH_McEvoy_abstract

Keywords: Ann Radcliffe, Matthew Lewis, Michael Kelly, Stephen Storace, Gothic Drama

ISBNs: 9781009532860 (HB), 9781009170376 (PB), 9781009170369 (OC)
ISSNs: 2634-8721 (online), 2634-8713 (print)

Contents

Introduction

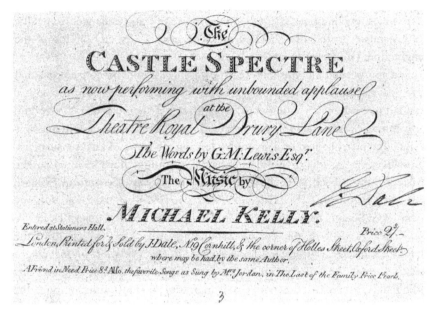

Figure 1 Title-page of Michael Kelly's vocal score (1798)
for Matthew Lewis's *The Castle Spectre*.
The Bodleian Libraries, University of Oxford, Mus. Voc. I, 103 (3)

This Element started accidentally, some years ago. I'd been asked to write a blog for the University of Stirling's Gothic Imagination site. Sitting in the British Library, it occurred to me that I could combine my interests in literature and music. As I happened to be reading Matthew Lewis's *The Castle Spectre* (1797) at the time, I ordered Michael Kelly's vocal score for the play (Figure 1). I was immediately taken with the text that arrived. A collection of popular numbers from a hit show, here arranged for piano, was winningly set out in easy-to-read (and easy-to-play) lines, its title page adorned with swirls and flourishes. Equally flamboyant in its rhetoric, it gleefully informed the reader that the work was 'now performing with unbounded applause at the Theatre Royal Drury Lane' (Kelly 1798: Title-page).

As I later wrote in the blog, what I was looking for when I ordered the music was some sense of its having been conceived of as Gothic – either through a deliberate historicism, a recourse to particular instruments (such as a glass harmonica), or the use of idioms associated with the music of *Sturm and*

Drang. I managed to find some implied 'ancientness' and duly reported on it but was otherwise frustrated in my search. I had been expecting what Isabella van Elferen has since called '*The Sounds of the Uncanny*'; instead, I found merry tunes, uncomplicated lines, and the music of transcendence. Ironically, Kelly's music profoundly shocked me. This wasn't, by any stretch of the imagination, Gothic music as I understood it.

I had approached the music of *The Castle Spectre* with preconceptions that were, in effect, misconceptions. Convinced I knew what Gothic music sounded like – how it should work, what affects it should cause – I overlaid Kelly's music with anachronistic expectations. I 'knew' that Gothic music is designed to provoke fear or discomfort, to trigger a sense of unease, suspense or dislocation. Asked to provide examples, I might have pointed to the insistent high-pitched screech of strings in the shower scene from Bernard Herrmann's score for Alfred Hitchcock's *Psycho* (1960); or the Requiem-gone-awry 'Ave Satani' theme of Jerry Goldsmith's music for Richard Donner's *The Omen* (1976); or the demonic-sounding organ runs which form the Phantom's motif in Andrew Lloyd Webber's *The Phantom of the Opera* (1986). I 'knew' that Gothic music is affect-driven, that it achieves its affects through its close association with Gothic narrative, that it signifies through the relationship it constructs with Gothic content, and that it might evoke particular 'Gothic' spaces or embed Gothic tropes. I 'knew' that contemporary Gothic music weirds other musical idioms, as does Paul Giovanni's folk score for Robin Hardy's *The Wicker Man* (1973) or Nick Cave and the Bad Seeds' song 'The Carny' (1986) with its ghastly fairground sound. Of course, I didn't expect *The Castle Spectre's* music to sound like the soundtracks for *The Wicker Man* or *Psycho*, but I did expect some kind of eighteenth-century equivalent. At the least, I thought that the music would present itself as 'Gothic', add to Gothic ambiance, accompany scenes that were meant to scare, and seek to induce Gothic affect. It didn't.

I started to chase up the music of other Gothic drama in the British Library, the Bodleian, the V&A's theatre archives and the National Library of Ireland, eventually amassing thousands of pieces. I quickly discovered that Gothic drama – which I'd started off by considering as a single category – came in very many different forms. It embraced musical plays, tragedies, comic operas, farces, melodramas, dramatic romances, operatic romances and numerous permutations of these terms, and this was just the spoken word drama. Embarrassed by the wealth of the material, I soon realised that I'd have to limit my research to spoken word drama. I also experienced another kind of embarrassment, as it dawned on me that *most* of the Gothic drama of the period came with music, but that for years I had let it slip under the radar.

I did, of course, sometimes come across the kind of music I expected to find. In the 'Cooper Family' collection in the V&A's theatre archives, I found Mr Nicholson's music (in manuscript) for John Walker's melodrama *The Wild Boy of Bohemia* (Olympic Theatre, London, 1827). It bore a striking resemblance to the music for a silent film. Cues marked 'Murder! Murder', 'Thy Temerity' and 'Help! Help', were accompanied by music that was recognisably 'Gothic', with cliff-hanger cadences, relentlessly agitated rhythms, and chords that provoked alarm and suspense (Nicholson 1827: Cues 9, 34 and 35). However, most of the music I discovered did not sound Gothic; it didn't seem even to want to engender Gothic affect. Much of it was jolly, some of it serene. There was a surprising amount of music sung by peasants and huntsmen engaged in innocent fun.

Reading and re-reading Gothic novels of the 1790s, I was struck afresh by the amount of music in them, not only in Ann Radcliffe's great novels of that decade, but also in Lewis's *The Monk* (1796) and a host of other works. They are full of heroines playing lutes, monks chanting, peasants piping and heroes serenading; even demons come with music. I realised that this too is not Gothic music. It might be achingly beautiful, stirring, transporting or mournful, but not sinister. Even the music of the supernatural – ghosts, witches and demons – is sweet. I found myself thinking, as Frits Noske had in 1981, 'it looks as if Gothic literature preceded Gothic music' (Noske 1981: 174). A number of questions soon came to my mind: If the music of the 1790s isn't seeking to create Gothic affect, what kind of affects is it aiming for? When had scary Gothic music come into being? Where had it happened first: on the stage or on the page? What is the relation between the imaginary music of the novels and the actual music of the Gothic dramas? Could looking at the real music of the Gothic drama help us to understand the imaginary music of the novels? How and when did the music of the Gothic become Gothic music?

The more music I played and read about, the more I grasped the complex and dynamic relation between the Gothic novels and drama of the period. It became evident that novels of the 1790s draw on comic opera, and that much 'Gothic drama' is essentially comic opera with imported content from Gothic novels. I realised too that the melodramatic music of the English stage had in turn an impact on music in Gothic fiction.

This Element traces music's transformation from sign of romance to underwriter of the Gothic, examining different stages on that journey. It looks at both the imagined music of novels and the actual music of Gothic drama and asks the same questions of each: What kind of music is featured? How does it signify within the text? What affects is it aiming to cause? Who (if anyone) is playing it? Who hears it? Does it signify differently to audiences/readers than to characters within the text? By and large, the Element proceeds chronologically but since it is both working within genres and thinking about the connections between them, there is some inevitable backtracking. More attention is given to the music of the first part of the period than to the latter, which has been better served by critics.

The first section looks at the imagined music of Gothic novels, positioning Radcliffe as the great pioneer in the field of musical Gothic, examining some of the innovative ways she employs musical discourse and tropes and arguing that music underwrites the romance of her imagined worlds. Section 2 considers responses to her music in the work of other novelists, most notably Eliza Fenwick and Matthew Lewis. Section 3 examines some of the ways Radcliffe imbeds operatic material and narrative techniques in her 1790s novels and offers some suggestions for hearing her music. The fourth section directs its attention to the actual music of the Gothic drama of the 1790s. It argues that much of what seems anomalous about many of the Gothic plays of the time can be traced back to their origins in a genre which to modern sensibilities seems almost antithetical to the Gothic drama: comic opera. The final part of the section considers operatic romances of the early nineteenth century. Section 5 looks at the music Michael Kelly produced for two of the best-known Gothic dramas of the period, drawing on contemporary accounts of the music's reception and its extra-theatrical life in order to get a fuller understanding of its affects, particularly those relating to the (real and pretend) supernatural. The final section presents some of the characteristic sounds of melodrama, with examples from *A Tale of Mystery* (1802) and *Ella Rosenberg* (1807), and outlines some of the ways in which melodramatic music differs from the music of previous Gothic drama. The Element finishes by considering some of the long-lasting effects of melodramatic music on Gothic fiction.

The Sound Files

Music is an integral part of most of the Gothic dramatic works of the period 1789–1820. Works which have no music, such as James Boaden's *The Secret Tribunal* (1795) and George Manners's *Edgar or Caledonian Feuds* (1806) (an adaptation of *The Castles of Athlin and Dunbayne*), are in a minority. However, despite its prevalence, music is all too easy for present-day readers of Gothic drama to ignore. In a prose play, lyrics can seem an excrescence, a decoration, a diversion from the main business of the work or an interpretive cul-de-sac; the temptation is to overlook or speed-read them. Sometimes play-wrights encourage readers to disregard or downgrade song lyrics. George Colman, for example, in his advertisement to *The Iron Chest* (1796), compares song lyrics unfavourably to '*lyrick Poetry*' and asserts that the play's 'Songs,

Duets, and Chorusses, are intended merely as vehicles for musical effect' (Colman 1796: xxii). Even when modern-day readers make the effort to read and assimilate lyrics, they do not know what the songs would have sounded like, how much stage time they might have taken, or what the impact on an audience would have been like when some of the most powerful and moving voices of the age filled the auditorium with them.

Hearing its music is vital for our understanding of the Gothic drama of the 1790s and the early nineteenth century, even more so for the drama of the 1790s than for the melodrama, which at least has a recognisably 'Gothic' sound. Approaching what we call Gothic drama through its music enables us to restore some of the fullness to texts we've made relatively impoverished because of our insistence on viewing them through what is essentially a reductive lens (the Gothic). It can help us move away from our preoccupation with the 'acoustics of horror' (to borrow Matt Foley's resonant phrase) and entertain a more nuanced understanding of drama of the period (Foley 2018: 460). It can also help illuminate long-running issues in criticism, casting light on what Diego Saglia, writing about Miles Peter Andrews' *The Mysteries of the Castle* (1795), calls its 'modal and tonal variations', 'generic fluidity and instability' (Saglia 2014: 232). Finally, thinking about the Gothic drama through music prompts questions about genre. What do we mean by the term Gothic drama? How useful a term is it? Which genres contribute to and neighbour Gothic drama?

I laid this project aside for some years because I was convinced that, for a work like this to make any sense, the music needed to be *heard* by its readers. There was no point in merely informing literary scholars that this music was not Gothic as we know it: the proof would be in the hearing and, then, I had no means of making such hearing possible. I believed – and still believe – that, to a large extent, the music featured in this Element speaks for itself and that, when it is heard, it can alter our conceptions of certain kinds of Gothic drama. Possibly more controversially, I also believe that hearing the music of the Gothic plays of the 1780s and 1790s can help us to 'hear' the imagined music of Gothic novels of the same period.

Eventually, two things enabled this work to come into being: the digital platform of the Elements series, and a grant from the British Academy and Leverhulme foundation. Receipt of the grant meant that the music I'd been researching could be arranged, performed live and recorded. It also funded the filming of a lecture-recital that I gave with the musicians featured in this Element at the Wallace Collection, London, in October 2022.[1]

The files you will hear represent some of the different contexts in which the music might originally have been heard. The song settings recreate performance in the domestic sphere or at a private concert. Most of the dramatic numbers have

---

[1] See www.youtube.com/watch?v=ZJmOPSVhXS0.

been arranged to represent performance in a theatre. Arrangement was necessary for a number of reasons, the primary one being that London theatre music of the period has fared badly in terms of preservation. On 24 February 1809, Drury Lane theatre was destroyed. Kelly describes in his *Reminiscences* how he had not only: 'the poignant grief of beholding the magnificent structure burning with merciless fury, but of knowing that all the scores of the operas which I had composed for the theatre, the labour of years, were then consuming: it was an appalling sight' (Kelly 1826: II, 281–82).

The previous year, Covent Garden theatre had also been destroyed by flames. If the fires destroyed much musical heritage, the disaster was compounded by 'Victorian librarians' who, as Roger Fiske notes, must have thrown away 'tattered scores and parts of operas they thought would never be produced again' (Fiske 1973: 582). For most of the music discussed in this Element, no full sets of orchestral parts remain. Despite the occasional exception (such as Matthew Peter King's manuscript for James Kenney's *Ella Rosenberg*), most of the theatre music under consideration here only survives in the form of vocal scores, such as that for *The Castle Spectre*.

Vocal scores were primarily aimed at amateur musicians. Their availability meant that theatrical numbers could travel into private houses (where they might form part of amateur productions), into concert halls, school rooms, parlours, drawing rooms, or out onto the street or into the fields. It wasn't always necessary to buy the complete score; frequently numbers could be purchased separately. Samuel Arnold's music for Boaden's *The Italian Monk* (1797) (not including the songs Arnold selected from existing repertoire by other composers) could be bought in its entirety for 6s. The four songs (though not the three-movement, six-page overture) were available separately at 1s apiece. Music could also be copied out by hand; Jane Austen's family, for example, transcribed the vocal score for *The Castle Spectre* into a family album.[2]

Most commonly, vocal scores contain vocal lines and a part for a piano, or less frequently, a harp. Sometimes a guitar or flute arrangement is supplied at the end – not necessarily in the same key. There is considerable variation between vocal scores in the amount of musical information given, in relation to harmony and original instrumentation. The level of detail informed our arrangement decisions. In the case of the 'Chorus of Nuns' from Arnold's music for *The Italian Monk*, for example, lack of detail (and lack of a chorus) meant that an arrangement for a smaller ensemble, representing a domestic or private performance, was preferable (Audio 2).

---

[2] See https://archive.org/details/austen1676477-2001/page/n93/mode/2up.

The ensemble recorded for this Element consists of keyboard, four strings, woodwind and vocalists; there is no brass or percussion. Though the two woodwind players were able to double up on instruments (which is why you can hear clarinet, flute, oboe and bassoon), you will never hear more than eleven musicians at any time. Obviously, such an ensemble does not equate to the forces – vocal or instrumental – that Drury Lane or Covent Garden had at their disposal. Fiske points out, that, from 1792, Drury Lane 'could accommodate a full Haydn-Mozart orchestra with eight woodwind, four brass, drums, and strings' (Fiske 1973: 281). King's manuscript for *Ella Rosenberg*, which was performed at Drury Lane in 1807, shows him writing for a full string section, woodwind, trombone, trumpets and horns, with percussion including drums in D, and a carillon (a set of bells). Not all theatres and all productions could muster such resources. Our ensemble arrangements represent those for a provincial playhouse of medium size, or for an amateur production in a wealthy household.

As resources would only enable the recording of approximately an hour's worth of music, rigorous selection was necessary. Sometimes deciding what would not be included was not difficult. Much of the music I collected bears the signs of being composed at short notice, with composers supplying only the most rudimentary, generic pieces. More often, my decision *was* difficult. My final selection was guided by the following considerations: I knew I needed examples from the most celebrated literary works (for example, *The Castle Spectre* and Samuel Taylor Coleridge's *Remorse* (1813)), as well as those notable for their paradigm-shifting music (such as Thomas Busby's for *A Tale of Mystery*); I wanted examples from a broad range of genres (song settings as well as Gothic dramas, melodramas, operatic romances, etc.); I needed examples of different kinds of numbers within these genres; I also hoped to represent the best-known composers working in the field and as many of London's theatrical venues as possible, while still giving precedence to Drury Lane and Covent Garden – theatres that attracted some of the best writing and drew the largest crowds. Finally, it was important to give examples of the kinds of songs and sounds associated with some of the familiar characters and situations of the Gothic novel. Thus, you will hear the songs of banditti, heroines, imprisoned heroes, poachers, peasants, boatmen, witches, nuns, retainers, a gypsy and a ghost, as well as storm music, evening numbers and music for the casting of spells. Where I had to choose within a *type* of number, I usually went for the most interesting examples. Sometimes, however, the need to have a piece that represented the work of a particular composer active in the field, or that came from a theatre otherwise unrepresented, took precedence over what I thought was more musically interesting.

Figure 2 John Braham with Harriet Abrams and her daughters, Harriet (the composer) (front left) and Theodosia (front right) by Richard Cosway (c. 1800). Permission Alamy Images.

There are inevitably some omissions; my most lamented is Thomas Attwood. One of the giants of the latter part of the period, Henry Bishop, is underrepresented (there is only one short number from *The Maniac or The Swiss Banditti* (1810)), but I direct readers to the *Romantic-Era Songs* site which has a great performance of his and Isaac Pocock's melodrama *The Miller and His Men* (1813).[3] As it was late in the day before I realised the significance of John O'Keeffe and Arnold's *The Castle of Andalusia*, there is nothing from that work. There are, however, selections from a host of composers, most of whom are unfamiliar now but whose acquaintance I hope you enjoy making as much as I have: Harriet Abrams (Figure 2), Samuel Arnold, Henry Bishop, John Braham (Figure 2), Thomas Busby, John Clarke-Whitfield, Charles Horn, Michael Kelly, Matthew Peter King, James Sanderson, William Shield and Stephen Storace.

1 'Various and Enchanting Powers': Music in the Radcliffean Romance

Though they are full of atmospheric sound effects, the earliest Gothic novels have very little interest in music. Horace Walpole's *The Castle of Otranto* (1764) merely has trumpets sounding challenges and Manfred proposing 'to waste some hours

---

[3] See www.sjsu.edu/faculty/douglass/music/album-miller.html.

of the night in music and revelling' (Walpole 2014: 55, 56, 60, 99), while music in Clara Reeve's *The Old English Baron* (1778) is confined to martial trumpets and a character who sings 'old songs' (Reeve 2003: 11, 86, 53). Fast-forward to the turn of the century and Gothic novels are full of music. They have titles like *The Nocturnal Minstrel* (1810). Even *Otranto*-inspired novels, like Stephen Cullen's *The Haunted Priory* (1794), with its outsize apparition with a giant helmet, come accompanied by music (Cullen 1794: 127). Otranto collapses to the sound of thunder, but at the spectacular fall of the ruined priory, 'music the most heavenly struck up', 'the De Profundis' is 'chanted by voices more than human, and the whole fabric shook with the notes of an organ' (126). *The Haunted Priory* also features the 'soft music' of an imprisoned, older woman, with a 'voice, as sweet as that of seraphs,' who, accompanying herself on a guitar, sings 'by snatches the most tender, melancholy notes' (204). Likewise, Sarah Green's *The Carthusian Friar* (1814) has a musical prisoner, though this time the gender is reversed; the player of 'melody from the fine full-toned organ … seemingly touched by a masterly hand' is a supposedly 'deceased Count' (Green 1814: III, 85). In Mrs F Isaacs's *Glenmore Abbey* (1805), music associated with maternal disappearance emanates from the thrilling acoustic setting of a cave. The novel's musical heroine (who plays 'a plaintive air on her guitar' whilst on a 'moss-grown rock') has the nous to realise that the music disturbing the servants is not supernatural (Isaacs 1805: I, 49). 'It is a very musical spirit,' said Ellen 'for I am now quite certain that the sounds were not imaginery [*sic*], and that it was a harp played with no common degree of execution' (II 205).

The musicality of Gothic novels of the period can also be seen in their cultural penumbra, or extra-textual reach. Gothic novels spawn song settings. James Hook set 'Ah Gentle Hope' the 'favourite sonnett' [*sic*] from Regina Maria Roche's *The Children of the Abbey* (1796), Krumpholtz (either Jean-Baptiste or Anne-Marie) set 'The Nun's Complaint' from Mary Robinson's *Vancenza* (1792), and both John Percy and John Clarke-Whitfield set Count Morano's song in Radcliffe's *The Mysteries of Udolpho*. Here is the first of the two verses of Clarke-Whitfield's setting (Audio 1).

Audio 1 John Clarke-Whitfield, first verse of 'Soft as the silver ray that sleeps' (1808) (setting of Count Morano's song from Ann Radcliffe's *The Mysteries of Udolpho*). Sung by Guy Cutting, accompanied by Seb Gillot. This audio is licensed under a CC BY-NC-ND 4.0 licence. Audio file is also available at www.cambridge.org/McEvoy

---

'Enchanting Powers of Expression'

Ann Radcliffe is the catalyst for the radical musicalisation of second-generation Gothic. Music is prominent amongst the few biographical details handed down

Figure 3 Emily playing the lute in Longman's 1806 edition of Radcliffe's
The Mysteries of Udolpho.
© The Trustees of the British Museum

about her. Her obituary notes that her 'chief delights' were '[t]o contemplate the
glories of creation' and 'to listen to fine music' (Anonymous 1824: 99). Thomas
Noon Talfourd remarks, '[t]o music she was passionately attached, and sang
herself with exquisite taste, though her voice, remarkably sweet, was limited in

compass'; he informs us that she went to performances of Handel oratorios, and loved sacred music', but could also be found '[a]t the Opera', where 'she was a frequent visitor, and on her return home would sit up singing over the airs she had heard, which her quickness of ear enabled her to catch, till a late hour' (Radcliffe 1826: I, 99).

There is, of course, no necessary link between a writer's being a musician and their making music a part of their literary art; Walpole for example enjoyed Italian opera, but music plays no large part in his Gothic novel. He was, however, writing a generation earlier. In the period between *Otranto* and Radcliffe's major novels, writing about music takes on a richness tempting to a writer of romance who is inclined to innovation. Radcliffe draws on the work of poets such as James Beattie, William Collins and James Thomson, where music is a fertile signifier, directing her readers' attention to these influences through her epigraphs. She shows herself to be au fait with the musical theorizing of writers such as Charles Avieson and Beattie. She also takes from the novel tradition, with its rich traditions of depicting female musicians and its inventive use of scenarios featuring private and public performance.

In Radcliffe's novels of the 1790s, music is not merely alluded to, nor simply encountered in the action. Musical cues conjure up setting and atmosphere, underwrite character and set up relationships; they are imbedded in her works' narrative strategies and carefully attended to in her poetic prose. The significance of music in Radcliffe is such that Walter Scott considers it a defining feature of her work. Writing in 1827 of the 'species of romance which Mrs Radcliffe introduced', he finds it 'bears nearly the same relation to the novel that the modern anomaly entitled a melodrame does to the proper drama' (Scott 1906: 320). Scott is not using the term 'melodrame' to signify a Gothic-leaning work with sensational content. Instead, he uses the word in its original sense, which signifies drama with music (*melos*) added. For Scott, the Radcliffean romance is the meeting-point of music and the novel.

The journey towards the comprehensive musicalisation that characterises *The Mysteries of Udolpho* (1794) progresses gradually. Radcliffe's first novel, *The Castles of Athlin and Dunbayne* (1789) exploits the associations of the lute with love and chaste female expressivity and uses musical performance as an indicator of emotion, but music itself is treated perfunctorily here in comparison with her later novels. The next novel, *A Sicilian Romance* (1790) contains much more music. Here Radcliffe draws more thoroughly on the discourse of sentimental literature, in which, as Pierre Dubois points out, music 'acquired a central role' because its 'mode of existence and diffusion was perfectly at one with the way affections and feelings were thought to work' (Dubois 2015: 84). The novel's heroine and hero are both described through this musicalised discourse. Julia's body, an indicator of her exquisite, natural sensibility; is set up both to respond to and express music. She is 'uncommonly susceptible of the charms of harmony. She had feelings which trembled in unison to all its various and enchanting powers' (Radcliffe 1993: 4). Her 'enchanting powers of expression ... seemed to breathe a soul through the sound' (4–5). Julia's lute is an extension of her very self; 'its tender notes accorded well with the sweet and melting tones of her voice' (5). Her lover's playing is similarly expressive, though rendered masculine; he plays 'a wild and melancholy symphony' with 'a masterly hand' (23). A description of his singing fuses the language of enchantment, emotion, affectivity and physically grounded ideality: his 'voice of more than magic expression swelled into an air so pathetic and tender, that it seemed to breathe the very soul of love' (23).

In *A Sicilian Romance*, Radcliffe uses music to highlight the social sympathies which govern the imagined world, as can be seen when Julia, her lover and her brother perform at a highly anachronistic concert (the characters play instruments that have not yet been invented: the 'piana-forte', the 'German flute' and the cello) (Radcliffe 1993: 22). In novels of manners, the topos of the concert, where emotion and display are to be found in close proximity, is frequently associated with emotional and even moral peril. In Elizabeth Inchbald's *A Simple Story* (1791), for example, the heroine's emotions are uncomfortably exposed as she plays the wrong notes at a concert, when the man she loves enters the room. In Maria Edgeworth's *Belinda* (1801), a novel with a woman's suspected sexual immorality at its heart, the music room is a problematic semi-public space within the domestic sphere. Significantly, the Radcliffean romance has no equivalent of the adulterous music trope. At the concert in *A Sicilian Romance*, artless music inevitably conveys truth. Julia is singing and accompanying herself on the piano when 'her voice resting on one note, swelled into a tone so exquisite, and from thence descended to a few simple notes, which she touched with such impassioned tenderness that every eye wept to the sounds' (Radcliffe 1993: 22). A 'pause of silence' indicates the audience's appreciation of this moment of shared experience (22). They eventually awaken from the 'moment of enchantment' but Hippolitus trembles in his flute-playing and 'forgot to play' (22). His silence amidst the 'general applause' is indicative of his exemplary response and shows that he is still under the sweet singer's guileless enchantments (22).

'Magic Echoes'

In Radcliffe's third novel, *The Romance of the Forest* (1791), the power of music is almost irresistible. As Beattie notes, 'certain melodies and harmonies have *an aptitude* to raise certain passions, affections, and sentiments, in the human soul'

(Beattie 1776: 455). For the heroine, Adeline, this aptitude is downright danger-
ous when the Marquis – who has had her kidnapped – attempts to seduce her by
masterminding a musical event characterised by superb acoustic engineering.
A melody is sung by 'a female voice, accompanied by a lute, a hautboy, and a few
other instruments,' which is then taken up into the larger performed landscape by
a horn (Radcliffe 1986a: 157). Adeline 'insensibly became soothed and interested; a tender melancholy stole upon her heart, and subdued every harsher
feeling' (157). The music is spell-like; 'the moment the strain ceased, the
enchantment dissolved, and she returned to a sense of her situation' (157).

More positive aspects of the power of music are rehearsed in the novel's
rewriting of a favoured scenario: the hero emerging to the song of the heroine.
The scene had featured in *A Sicilian Romance*, but its occurrence in *Forest* sees
a much more comprehensive integration of musical language and the language
of the passions. Adeline, wandering outside the confines of the castle, finds
solace in 'a dewy glade, whose woods, sweeping down to the very edge of the
water, formed a scene ... sweetly romantic' (Radcliffe 1986a: 75). She sits
'inspired ... with that soft and pleasing melancholy, so dear to the feeling
mind ... and then, in a voice whose charming melody was modulated by the
tenderness of her heart, she sung the following words' (75). Music acts as
a guarantor of taste and virtue, promising an index of the soul. Adeline is
inspired by, even at one with, nature, and her exquisite music-making is linked
to her being such a perfectly set up organism; her vocal performance gives
evidence of her 'natural' sensibilities. Her voice reveals her moral nature; its
'melody' is 'modulated by the tenderness of her heart'.

At this point, Radcliffe picks up on a motif found in Sophia Lee's *The Recess*
(1786). In Lee's novel, as the sister-heroines are wandering outside their home,
Matilda 'discovered in the hollow of the wood and building, a very fine echo'
and 'delighted', starts to sing; 'the notes dying distinctly away, formed
a melancholy symphony' after which a 'voice, that sunk at once from my ear
to my heart, conjured me in the most earnest manner to stop' (Lee 1786: I, 90).
Lee's echo summons the hero who then interrupts the heroine. Radcliffe
approaches the echo motif in a more sustained fashion.

> A distant echo lengthened out her tones, and she sat listening to the soft
> response, till repeating the last stanza of the Sonnet, she was answered by
> a voice almost as tender, and less distant. She looked round in surprise, and saw
> a young man in a hunter's dress, leaning against a tree, and gazing on her with
> that deep attention, which marks an enraptured mind. (Radcliffe 1986a: 76)

Adeline sings; an echo follows; the audible echo gives way to another kind of
echo, a male version of herself with a voice 'almost as tender'. The echo has

worked a strange kind of textual magic, bringing into narrative existence the novel's love interest in a manner akin to a spirit-raising.

In *The Recess*, the echo is literal. Echoes in *The Romance of the Forest* are more than mere sounds. The echo is the structuring principle at work in a universe governed by correspondence and divine sympathy. Echoes pervade the novel. They sound over lakes and rocks. The novel finishes with a dance at the lakeside when the mountains 'answered only to the strains of mirth and melody' (Radcliffe 1986a: 362). Echoes in the novel enable the unsayable to be said and create bonds between characters. When Adeline finishes singing her lyric, 'Titania to her love', 'she immediately heard repeated in a low voice' lines she has just sung (285, 286). Adeline writes poems that foreground echoes. 'Morning, on the Seashore', which features music that conjures up the fairies 'festive rites', has the lines: 'Bid Music's voice on Silence win,/Till magic echoes answer round' (289). Earlier, an echo features in a passage notable for its seamless blending of feeling into music, and prose into poetry. At sunset amidst the mountains, Adeline gazes 'with a kind of still rapture' on the lakes before her (261). The passage passes from her emotional experience of the scene to a quotation from Thomson's *The Seasons*, at which point Radcliffe describes 'the mellow and enchanting tones' of a French horn making its way across the water (262). Although we know that the sound relates to a pleasure boat carrying a party of foreign tourists, in its psychological resonances it is an extension of the preceding elements: Adeline's state of mind, Thomson's poem and the ambiance of the scene. In a typical moment of blending, the tenor of the scene is sustained in a poem by Adeline which references its own echoic nature. 'How sweet that strain of melancholy horn!/ That floats along the slowly-ebbing wave,/And up the far-receding mountains borne,/Returns a dying close from Echo's cave!' (263).

'A Strain of Such Tender and Enchanting Sweetness'

Where Radcliffe weaves music into her novels with impressive depth, intensity and level of detail, her imitators are not always so convincing. In Eleanor Sleath's *The Orphan of the Rhine* (1798), Laurette and her lover are chastely courting in the countryside. Despite surface similarities to Radcliffe's work, the sonic motifs function merely as a shorthand, connoting the requisite atmosphere in which a pure and devoted young love is presumed to grow. The lovers, 'under the thick shade of an oak or a plane tree', 'would frequently pass many hours listening to the harmony of the birds'; Laurette, the musical heroine, seats herself 'upon a stile or a fragment of rock' to play 'some charming air' upon her lute 'which she knew how to touch with exquisite pathos'; the landscape is supplemented by human music – 'the distant murmur of a waterfall gave a soothing tranquillity to the scene, whose monotony was only occasionally interrupted by the lively tones of the oboe, or the pipe of the shepherd' (Sleath 1968: 124). In Radcliffe's work such a scene would not be so generalised, the characters would not listen for hours to bird song, the waterfall would not be monotonous nor the oboe lively. Instead, her characters would be embedded within a more particularised scene, whose sounds would communicate much about the characters' emotions, memories, desires, their relation to the divine, and to the wider world around them.

By *Forest* and *The Mysteries of Udolpho*, Radcliffe employs music to serve a dizzying variety of narrative purposes. Musicality reveals morality (*Udolpho*'s villain Montoni has no time for music). It provides a gateway to transcendental experience. As Dubois points out, music, particularly religious music, is the means through which Radcliffe brings into being a 'feminine form of sublime' which goes 'beyond the Burkean dichotomy', divorcing the sublime from fear (Dubois 2015: 163). In these novels, the sounds of nature correspond to (and continue from) human music, revealing what Alison Milbank calls 'the moral beauty of the created order' (Milbank 2014: 98). As Ahmet Süner points out, Radcliffe also uses music as a 'structural element, as the means of shifting between narrative modes or creating 'narrative suspense' (Süner 2020: 450, 455). Music, also, as Dubois writes, 'performs a crucial role in Radcliffe's endeavor to represent psychological states' (Dubois 2015: 162). Disappearing sound proves to be an effective means for thinking about the nature of perception. As Noelle Chao points out 'No other fiction writer from this period assigned music such a significant and diverse role' (Chao 2013: 85).

Crucially, music performs a coalescing function, fundamental to Radcliffe's creation of a world characterised by integration and harmony. It effects a wider sense of coherence and union, integrating the potentially disparate elements of scenes. In a passage in *Forest*, the music of a 'solitary sailor, leaning with crossed arms against the mast' triggers the process. His 'mournful ditty' heard across 'the sounding waters' is consonant with and amplifies the visual elements of the seascape, creating a synaesthetic effect (Radcliffe 1986a: 293). Adeline is then inspired to write a poem, 'Night', which again casts the scene as a soundscape. Shortly afterwards, music is associated with an experience of transcendence. A 'strain of such tender and entrancing sweetness stole on the silence of the hour, that it seemed more like celestial than mortal music' (295). In harmony with nature, the swell of its 'undulating sounds' suggest the sea (295). When the song is interrupted and transformed by the fluctuations of the breeze, Adeline encounters something that is even more ideal. 'Sometimes the breeze wafted [the sounds] away, and again returned them in tones of the most languishing softness. The links of the air thus broken, it was music rather than melody that she caught' (295).

'In Harmony with the Temper of Her Mind'

The Mysteries of Udolpho announces its commitment to music from the very first chapter, much of which takes place in a music room. (Readers of *Forest* had to wait until chapter five for their first music.) Music is so continually present in *Udolpho* that its absence signifies strongly. It is a work in which music is overwhelmingly a signifier of the good. There is no equivalent of the passage in the previous novel where, in the Rousseauian Protestant paradise of the La Lucs, over-indulgence in music necessitates self-discipline.

Whereas the treatment of much of the music of Radcliffe's earlier works is premised upon its irresistible affectivity, something rather more interesting is going on in *Udolpho*. At many points, rather than music working on the heroine, it seems that the heroine creates a music that corresponds to her. In one passage, Emily is enjoying the melancholy and beauty of an evening by the shore. The moon throws an 'extending line of radiance ... upon the waters, the sparkling oars, the sail faintly silvered' and we are told that 'Emily's spirits were in harmony with this scene' (Radcliffe 1986b: 541). At this metaphorical reference to 'harmony', actual music commences: '[a]s she sat meditating, sounds stole by her on the air, which she immediately knew to be the music and the voice she had formerly heard at midnight' (541–2).

Emily also brings music into being in an earlier passage. Her feelings, the landscape and her memories are tightly integrated when she sits:

> after supper at a little window, that opened upon the country, observing an effect of the moon-light on the broken surface of the mountains, and remembering that on such a night as this she once had sat with her father and Valancourt, resting upon a cliff of the Pyrénées, she heard from below the long-drawn notes of a violin, of such tone and delicacy of expression, as harmonized exactly with the tender emotions she was indulging, and both charmed and surprised her. (168)

Emily starts the scene as a connoisseur of a picturesque effect. As she begins to reminisce, the *Merchant of Venice* allusion establishes an idyllic resonance, and music comes into being. Not only does the music harmonise with Emily's emotions, conveying her tone of mind, it almost seems to have been conjured up by Emily's mind.

The world of *Udolpho* is one of exceptional integration in which, at peak moments, music, landscape and memory become almost interchangeable. In the episode that Emily is recalling in the previous passage, Valancourt points out that 'scenes' can 'soften the heart, like the notes of sweet music, and inspire that delicious melancholy which no person ... would resign for the gayest pleasures' (Radcliffe 1986b: 46). St. Aubert agrees '"Yes," said he, with an half-suppressed sigh, 'the memory of those we love – of times for ever past! in such an hour as this steals upon the mind, like a strain of distant music in the stillness of night; – all tender and harmonious as this landscape, sleeping in the mellow moon-light' (46). The passage is characterised by a spilling-over of vocabulary from the language of visual response, music and emotion: landscape 'scenes' first work on the perceiving subject in a manner akin to 'sweet music'; the language of softening, associated with musical response, is then used of a visual scene; memory is figured as 'a strain of distant music', and the landscape is described as 'harmonious'.

Later that evening, the image evoked by St Aubert is reworked, becoming textual reality. Emily, concerned about her father, looks into the

> still and beautiful night, the sky was unobscured by any cloud, and scarce a leaf of the woods beneath trembled in the air. As she listened, the mid-night hymn of the monks rose softly from a chapel, that stood on one of the lower cliffs, an holy strain, that seemed to ascend through the silence of night to heaven. (Radcliffe 1986b: 47)

At the moment of sacred contemplation, St Aubert's figurative language becomes actuality. He talked of memory in terms of the landscape and music. When Emily thinks of her father, music arises from the landscape. His metaphorical harmony becomes narrative reality, in the form of a midnight chant ascending to 'heaven' and taking Emily's thoughts with it.

If the sound world of *Forest* could be said to derive from the figure of the echo, that of *Udolpho* is, as Joanna Kokot has argued, informed by the concept of harmony. Kokot points to the 'inner harmony of the protagonist, which resonates with the harmony of the world around her', 'the "horizontal" harmony of the communal existence' and its 'vertical aspect', associated with the divine (Kokot 2015: 64, 59, 60). Many aspects contribute to the creation of harmony in *Udolpho*. As Jakub Lipski points out, it is partly derived from Radcliffe's habits of ekphrasis, of figuring images that create a 'natural union of the visual and the audible' and 'foreshadow the Romantic idea of the total work of art uniting literature, music and painting' (Lipski 2015: 11, 3). *Udolpho*'s harmony is also indebted to Radcliffe's use of musicalised discourse, her extensive sharing and transferring of epithets, and her surprising refusal to let a musical metaphor remain merely figurative.

When Radcliffe writes about 'harmony' she is often blending the visual and auditory (as well as the emotional). At times the usage is very subtle, as when seated watching the Mediterranean in 'melancholy dejection', the 'hollow murmur and the obscuring mists, that came in wreaths up the cliffs gave a solemnity to the scene, which was in harmony with the temper of [Emily's] mind' (Radcliffe 1986b: 558). In such a passage, the harmony is not only between Emily's mind and the landscape, but also between the aural and visual elements. Radcliffe subtly references musical discourse by using the word 'temper'. Her prose is carefully calibrated, her musical terms deployed unobtrusively. *Udolpho* has a delicately suggestive web of emotionally and spiritually relevant musical language. If we look to Matthew Lewis's prose by way of contrast, an 'air' is an 'air'. When Lewis writes about 'harmony' in *The Monk* he does so, for the most part, in a way that is not metaphorical but strictly musical. In Radcliffe, the word 'harmony' very rarely only refers to music but is also connected to a range of other usages of the word, to her heroines' mien, for example, or to atmosphere both physical and moral. Radcliffe's musical vocabulary resonates within many spheres simultaneously. She uses musical words in contexts where they are both metaphorical and musical, and where they blend into moral and aesthetic discourses. Moreover, Radcliffe seldom commits to a purely metaphorical use of her musical terminology. Crucially the terms are usually grounded in the physical world in which the heroine is situated. She rarely refers to harmony unless actual sound is either present or implied. Harmony is both metaphorical and literal.

Radcliffe's most memorable achievement for many of her contemporaries was her ability to conjure up what William Hazlitt describes as 'all that is obscure, visionary, and objectless in the imagination' (Hazlitt 1899: 171), and to transport her readers to what Coleridge terms as 'the very edge and confines of the world of spirits' (Townshend and Wright 2014: 8). In recent times, our habit has been to look to the sublime as the repository for the 'obscure', 'visionary' and 'the world of spirits'. However, the sublime forms only one part of the enchantment of *Udolpho*. The novel is 'objectless' and 'visionary' because Radcliffe's prose (and poems) are profoundly concerned with synthesising. The world of *Udolpho* (outside the residences of villains such as Montoni) is a rich fantasy world of blending and magical thinking. It is a 'fairy' place, uniquely sympathetic to its heroines, where it is possible to leave the earthly and come back again, where, as Terry Castle says, 'Magical reunion is possible. Thoughts shape reality . . . [and] wishes seem to come true' (Castle 1995: 128).

Music underwrites the magic of Radcliffe's romances. It is the element that makes possible what Talfourd calls her possession of the 'enchanted land' of romance (Radcliffe 1826: 10, 11). It is no accident that Radcliffe so frequently uses the terms 'magic' and 'enchantment' of music: evocative and associative, music stimulates memory and recovers those who are absent. It brings into narrative existence scenes which take their cue from the heroine's mind. As Emily discovers at the end of *Udolpho*, the mere intent to play music can bring characters into being. She takes her lute to 'the fishing-house . . . that she might again hear there the tones, to which St. Aubert and her mother had so often delighted to listen' (99). Although she abandons the playing, listening instead to 'the mournful sighing of the breeze', the narrative logic means that Valancourt is conjured into existence (100).

In *Udolpho*, music is central to the aesthetic of blending and harmony, of repletion and sympathy. This is a world where landscape, self and music reinforce each other, where the literal and metaphorical are not separate levels. Music guarantees the Providential outcomes of a world in which Montonis have no harmony and will ultimately fail.

2 'No Longer Blended': Rewriting Radcliffe's Music

Radcliffe's contemporaries realised the significance of music in her work. As Dale Townshend and Angela Wright point out, they make 'metaphorical associations between Ann Radcliffe and the metaphorical figure of the nightingale, Philomela'; the obituarist in the *Edinburgh Review*, for example, referring to her as 'the sweet bird that sings its solitary notes, shrowded [*sic*] and unseen' (Townshend and Wright 2014: 3). When her contemporaries pastiche her work, they foreground her musicality. The doleful humour of Coleridge's 'Ode, in Mrs Ratcliff's manner' (1800), derives from a *Udolpho*-like interpenetration of song, landscape and emotion. A voice sings something 'In melody most like an old Sicilian song'; a listener takes on the singer's emotions, and the landscape is imbued by the singer's desolation: 'That night there was no moon!!' (Coleridge 2022: 11, 8 and 51).

Radcliffe's musical language and figures are equally available to those who wish to counter her mode of romance. Sometimes the rewriting of Radcliffean scenarios is fairly superficial. Francis Lathom's *Astonishment!!!* (1801), for example, gains mileage by eroticising the association of the love object and music. This figure has a long precedent (see Jacques Cazotte's *Le diable amoureux* (1772) as an example) but it becomes particularly perverse in the wake of Radcliffe's notably chaste scenes. Lathom establishes a transgressive frisson when a female, 'the most beautiful imagination could conceive', lies on a 'bed of roses' accompanied by 'strains of music' which grow 'louder and sweeter' (Lathom 1802: I, 170). A male musician is similarly eroticised in Ann Julia Hatton's *Secret Avengers* (1815). The 'restless eyes' of a desiring adulterous woman fall 'on the recumbent figure of Albert' sleeping at the base of a pillar with a flute and a 'roll of music' by his feet (Hatton 1815: III, 133). Like Lathom's sleeper, Albert is pictured in relation to the natural world, though here the effects are somewhat comical: a 'large beautiful butter-fly . . . several times settled on his lips and eyelids, and fluttered round his face, without disturbing him' (III, 135).

Eliza Fenwick's *Secresy or, The Ruin on the Rock* (1795) is a more thorough-going attempt to deconstruct the Radcliffean romance. Fenwick determinedly and dexterously short-circuits Radcliffe's musical scenarios and language to construct an unsympathetic world in which Sibella, her heroine, who is possessed of genius and great sensibility, is doomed. The excursion described by Sibella's friend, Caroline Ashburn, is an early example. Fenwick reworks a passage in *Udolpho* where a party enjoys 'a collation of fruit and coffee' while some 'horns, placed in a distant part of the woods, where an echo sweetened and prolonged their melancholy tones, broke softly on the stillness of the scene' (Radcliffe 1986b: 481). Whereas the passage in *Udolpho* is an image of innocent diversion, the corresponding passage in *Secresy* functions as an image of a hyper-stimulated, pampered society. There are '[i]ces, the choicest fruits, and other delicate preparations for the refreshment of the palate … Horns, clarionets, and bassoons are stationed in a neighbouring grove, with their sweet concords occasionally to soothe our fatigues … notwithstanding all this costly care', Caroline acidly notes, 'it is very possible we shall pass a listless morning' (Fenwick 1989: 40).

In a later passage, Fenwick powerfully rewrites one of Radcliffe's favoured scenarios – the heroine singing in nature and meeting the hero – to devastating effect. Sibella, like Radcliffe's Adeline, is fond of venturing outside her Gothic prison to sing in the surrounding landscape. Doing so one night, she looks on the 'glittering surface (made resplendent by the moon's reflection)' of a 'small and beautiful lake', commenting that '[a]ll seemed in union with my mind' though noting that while 'an undisturbed serenity reigned through nature … a tumult of delight claimed its share' in her breast (127). The Radcliffean mode with its luxuriant prose is then abruptly terminated. The next sentence is one of the shortest in the book: 'I sang' (127). Then, in a rude reminder that Sibella is not in a timeless present, the 'sound of two, from some very distant bell floated through the air' (127). Despite the potential of lakes in romance, Sibella is not within a world that echoes and reflects her. Her song does not generate a response which is the answer to her dreams and wishes, and her lover does not materialise. Instead, a very material object – a 'little white ball … several folds of paper, with a small pebble in the middle, to give it weight I suppose' – whizzes past her; it is the hero's love note (127–8). Fenwick's is a dismal and fallen reality, a disenchanted version of the Radcliffean romance.

If the rewriting of the Radcliffean musical meeting scene makes the fate of Sibella more striking and heart-rending, it also points up her lover, Murden's, tragedy. The incident is told twice in the novel, by Sibella herself and by Murden. He recalls that '[i]t was I think one of the finest nights I ever beheld; and I must have wanted that fervour of soul which gave birth to my love, had

I not been enchanted with the scene' (208). However, the scene quickly changes. The language of blending and sympathetic acoustics is negated: despite the 'resplendent moon', 'light and shade no longer blended but were abruptly contrasted. No cloud glided into motion, no zephyr into sound' (208, 209). In this moment of contrast and clarity, the weeping Murden makes 'a vow at the shrine of reason to abandon my mad enterprize, to quit for ever and ever this seductive rock' (209). His resolve, however, is abandoned when, like a siren, Sibella sings. 'Alas reason and resolution were instantaneously torn from me, by the sweetest sound that ever stole on the listening ear of night' (209). Murden's inability to read the signs of anti-romance mean that, ultimately, his reason, his will, and his life – as well as Sibella's – are forfeit.

'With a Hand Bold and Rapid': Matthew Lewis's *The Monk*

The most thoroughgoing demolition of Radcliffean music is to be found in Lewis's *The Monk*. 'With a hand bold and rapid' serves as a good description of his technique.

THE MONK.

While she sung. Ambrosio listened with delight.

Figure 4 Matilda playing the harp in a French edition of *The Monk* (Printed for Theophilus Barrois, Paris, 1807). Courtesy of Yale University.

Like Radcliffe, Lewis was very musical. Margaret Baron-Wilson's *The Life and Correspondence of M. G. Lewis* (1839) informs us that he grew up in a musical household. His mother 'was in the habit of taking musical lessons from all the eminent professors of the day', and they 'had the constant *entrée* at her house' (Baron-Wilson 1839: I, 13). Lewis himself had a good musical education and fancied himself a critic at a very young age. An anecdote has him exclaiming in 'a shrill, tiny voice' 'That's a very fine movement!', to 'general mirth' at an 'evening concert' in the Lewis household (I, 12). As an adult, Lewis enjoyed the company of musicians and worked successfully with a number of composers. He also composed music himself and, as Baron-Wilson points out, 'many of his melodies met with very general applause' (I, 245). Lewis wrote the tunes for some of the numbers in his dramatic work including 'The wind it blows cold' in *Adelmorn the Outlaw* (I, 248–9) and the lullaby in *The Castle Spectre* (Audio 13), which appeared (in a longer version) in his *Twelve Ballads* (1808).

Music is exposed to sustained and extensive rewriting in *The Monk*. In Elvira's back-story, where the prototypical narrative of the unequal marriage undesired by the parents of the bride goes horribly wrong, musical references serve not to console but to signpost the unfolding tragedy. Elvira is driven to tears 'when the Spanish Sailor chaunted some well-known air'; the speaker in Gonzalvo's poem 'The Exile', will no longer hear 'the well-known ditty/ Sung by some Mountain-Girl' (Lewis 1998: 214 and 216 ll. 29–30). Whereas Radcliffe's music strays over boundaries and has a tendency to infuse and permeate, to prove unlocatable or even inaudible, Lewis's music is nearly always located in a specific place. *The Monk* is interested in performance; it is specific about what and how its characters play and is alert to the practicalities of music-making. We see Matilda tuning a harp (before she 'preluded ... with ... exquisite taste') (Figure 4), Antonia putting her guitar back in its case, and Theodore – who is specifically hired as a musician – tuning his guitar and preparing 'to strike it' (75, 312, 287) (Figure 5).

When the Gypsy sings and dances in *The Monk*, it is a highly un-Radcliffean affair. Not only is it a solo rather than communal event, but rather than emerging from the surrounding landscape, it is introduced as a shattering of the prevailing atmosphere. Moreover, there is an unsettling equivalence between the Gypsy's spell-making and her body, between the 'variety of singular figures' she traces on the ground with what seems to be a magic rod and the 'eccentric attitudes of folly and delirium' she herself effects (34, 35). Here, as elsewhere, Lewis is interested in endings and discontinuities. The Gypsy 'broke off her dance', then 'whirled herself round thrice with rapidity', before leaving 'a moment's pause' before the song (35). Radcliffe songs tend to be lyrics: contiguous with the spirit of the romance world around them, descriptive of mood and atmosphere and

"But at least," said the old portoress, take
care not to sing any thing profane."

Figure 5 Theodore playing the guitar outside the convent in a French
edition of *The Monk* (Printed for Theophilus Barrois, Paris, 1807).
Courtesy of Yale University.

associated with individual expression, the Gypsy's song by contrast is a ballad
which serves – as the music of the inset dream does – as prophecy. In *The Monk*,
music is nearly always functional and transactional rather than expressive. The
Gypsy performs to make money; Matilda plays to seduce Ambrosio; Theodore
twice engages in some very un-Radcliffean loud singing, once outside the tower
where Agnes is imprisoned, and later outside the convent (Figure 5).

Aside from the prevalence of wicked music associated with demons and
witches, nowhere is Lewis's assault on the music of the romance world more
ostentatious than in his revision of the musical heroine. Antonia, with her 'tone
of unexampled sweetness', would at first seem to be a good fit for the role
(Lewis 1998: 9). Her beautiful voice, however, becomes the means of a vicious
attack on Radcliffean logic. Adeline in *Forest* might be saved by singing in her
sleep, but 'prayers breathed in tones of unequalled melody' do not save Antonia
from Ambrosio's depredations (379). On the contrary, they spur him onto rape.
The Radcliffean musical heroine is most powerfully subverted in the portrayal

of Matilda, an accomplished musician who seemingly channels her emotions into her affective art but is in fact a demonic manipulator. As Frits Noske points out, 'virtue and taste have separated' (Noske 1981: 170). Matilda's long and thrilling performance in the second chapter spells out some of the less innocent implications of the language of musical response in romance, particularly the terminology relating to captivation, enchantment and desire. When Matilda asks, 'shall I endeavour to amuse you with my Harp?' Ambrosio's response – 'I knew not that you understood Music' is only too apt (74). Matilda, a knowing performer, very well understands what music may achieve. Despite her protestations to the contrary, she is 'a perfect Mistress of the Instrument' (75). In Matilda, Lewis ruptures the discourse of innocence associated with the musical heroine. She manipulates the practicalities of performance to lascivious effect (Figure 4). 'Her Habit's long sleeve would have swept along the Chords of the Instrument: To prevent this inconvenience She had drawn it above her elbow, and by this means an arm was discovered formed in the most perfect symmetry, the delicacy of whose skin might have contended with snow in whiteness' (78). Matilda is performing in a dizzying number of ways; not only is she performing on her instrument, but she is also giving a performance as a Radcliffean heroine and a Shakespearean heroine (Viola), as well as playing on Ambrosio. After her prelude, she performs a 'soft and plaintive' air and Ambrosio 'felt his uneasiness subside, and a pleasing melancholy spread itself into his bosom'. At this point, she 'changed the strain' (75). The term 'strain', like so many of the musical terms in the passage, has an extra shade of meaning, not only designating the melody but also suggesting the sexual tension conjured up by Matilda. Having rendered Ambrosio receptive, she proceeds to arouse him, stirring him up with 'a few loud martial chords', played with 'an hand bold and rapid' (75).

It is no shock that the scene ends with sexual consummation. Since the opening of the novel, Lewis has increasingly revealed the double entendre implicit in the language of musical response. It is there in the 'melodious seduction' of Matilda's voice, or in Antonia's awareness that 'the sound of [Ambrosio's] voice seemed to penetrate into her very soul' (68, 18). The sexualisation of musical language continues throughout the text. When Ambrosio is sated with Matilda, we are told that 'her musical talents, which She possessed in perfection, had lost the power of amusing him' (235). Double entendre is employed most ostentatiously in the scene in which Ambrosio attempts to seduce Antonia. When he asks her whether she's met someone 'The sound of whose voice soothed you, pleased you, penetrated to your very soul?' (261), his language is an outrage on the romance reader's modesty (if not the uncomprehending Antonia's).

Music in *The Monk* communicates the text's eroticism, alerting readers not only to Antonia's desirability, but also to Theodore's, whose 'sweetness of . . . voice, and masterly manner of touching the Instrument' attracts the nuns of St Clare's convent (291). The charms of that 'amiable Boy' are again discussed in musical terms when Raymond tells Lorenzo that 'what rendered him most agreeable to me, was his having a delightful voice, and some skill in Music' (166). Music, or the lack of it, has much to say about the relative attractions of Agnes and Theodore. Although Agnes 'possessed several talents in perfection, particularly those of Music and drawing', she never demonstrates her musical talents (130). Rather, the enduring sounds associated with Agnes are the 'groans' she emits in the dungeon. (There are at least nine references to Agnes's groans in volume III, chapter iii.) Theodore and Agnes are often figured in parallel situations which highlight the musical potency of the former and the muteness of the latter. He is often found singing while she is imprisoned. At the convent, when Theodore hopes to hear Agnes respond to his ballad, 'No voice replied to his' (291). Locked in the tower by her aunt, Agnes's response is to let down a note with her escape plans. It's a nasty irony that her reply contains a piece of prescient wordplay. She writes of having 'an opportunity of concerting our future plans'; however, the only concert or musical entertainment for Raymond will be the songs of Theodore (145).

After *The Monk*

Lewis's *The Monk* inspired a new wave of novels that gleefully investigate the (temporary) triumphs of villainy in romance worlds. Charlotte Dacre's *Zofloya* (1806) and Percy Bysshe Shelley's *Zastrozzi* (1810) both bear the mark of Lewis but are committed to finding further ways of undermining the ingenuous tropes of Radcliffean romance. Not content with creating an anti-heroine, Victoria, who proves 'indifferent' to the 'wild beauties', of a 'soft gale' and the 'melody of the birds' and can dance even more deliriously than Lewis's gypsy, Dacre re-examines the language of enchantment associated with the trope of the expressive voice (Dacre 1997: 62). Victoria's nemesis, Zofloya, is a musical adept, 'highly skilled in the science of harmony', with 'honied accents' and a 'voice, like the sweet murmuring sound of an Aeolian harp, swept by the breath of the zephyr' (220, 156, 159). His, however, is not an enchanting but a 'fascinating voice' (the word derives from the Latin fascinare 'to bewitch') (236). It is associated not with concord but with the exercise of power and mind control; '[E]ven . . . ferocious banditti are tamed into submission' by it (236). In a particularly persuasive passage, Zofloya makes music on a boat; 'towering as a demi-god', he 'ravished the surrounding party with his exquisite harmony' (164). Dacre's language not only insinuates sexual predation but also the subjugation of nature: 'even the undulating waves, in the rapt ear of enthusiastic fancy, appeared to keep respectful music' (164). Elsewhere, Dacre presents a scene that both alludes to the abbey garden incident in *The Monk* and cleverly reworks Radcliffe's echo motif. Victoria is murderously soliloquising in a garden when a 'faint echo seemed to repeat her last words ... in a low, hollow tone, as if sounding at a distance, and borne by the wind' (146). When Zofloya appears, he claims his arrival is linked to the power of 'sympathy' and that Victoria's 'very *thoughts* have power to attract' him (178). However, rather than a case of Radcliffean virtuous sympathy, this is clearly a case of summoning the devil.

In *Zastrozzi*, Shelley proves himself less interested than either Lewis or Dacre in demonic forces; although possessed of diabolic genius, his Matilda is thoroughly human. He is, however, as intent as they are on untying the Radcliffean link between nature, music, virtue and sensibility. Shelley is specifically interested in acts of musical interpretation – and the opportunities for sabotage that they offer. His Matilda, like Lewis's, is a harpist. Her 'taste for music ... exquisite; her voice of celestial sweetness', she draws 'sounds of soul-touching melody from the harp' (Shelley 1986: 57). A manipulative genius, Matilda presents herself as a Radcliffean musical heroine to her dupe, Verezzi. Her deception is undoubtedly helped by Shelley's ability to create Radcliffean locales and wield Radcliffean musicalised language. Matilda leads Verezzi on a walk through a forest, where the 'craggy heights beyond might distinctly be seen, edged by the beams of the silver moon' (58). Entering 'a small tuft of trees', she makes 'sounds of such ravishing melody' that Verezzi thinks 'some spirit of the solitude had made audible to mortal ears ethereal music' (59). By her design, the 'music was in unison with the scene – it was in unison with Verezzi's soul' (59). Already 'struck' by Matilda's 'loveliness and grace, and fooled by her pretended 'sensibility', Verezzi is taken in by her consummate ability to stage a Radcliffean scene, complete with 'judicious arrangement of the music', reading it as a good romance reader should (59). He has 'no doubt in his mind but that, experiencing the same sensations herself, the feelings of his soul were not unknown to her' (59). Thus, is he doomed.

Arguably, the most thorough response to *The Monk*'s music is to be found in the work of Radcliffe herself. *The Italian* (1797) is a more wary novel than Radcliffe's earlier works, a novel by a writer who has learned from *The Monk* that she cannot necessarily trust in the good faith of her readers. In it, she turns from the syntheses of *Udolpho*. *The Italian* has insincere and misleading music; it is even, for a substantial portion, without music. However, it is also the work in which Radcliffe brings to its height another of her grand musical innovations: writing the novel as opera.

3 Ann Radcliffe Goes to the Opera

Throughout her novels of the 1790s, Radcliffe is committed to sonic innovation. In *Udolpho* she invents the concept of 'picturesque sounds' (a phenomenon which, like the original picturesque, lies partway between the beautiful and the sublime, between art and nature, and relies on the idea that occluded distance stimulates the imagination). In an uncharacteristically intrusive moment, the implied author intervenes to excuse the unfamiliarity of the paradoxical term that has just been coined, signalling it with italics.

> The scene was filled with that cheering freshness, which seems to breathe the very spirit of health, and she heard only sweet and *picturesque* sounds, if such an expression may be allowed – the matin-bell of a distant convent, the faint murmur of the sea-waves, the song of birds, and the far-off low of cattle, which she saw coming slowly on between the trunks of trees. (Radcliffe 1986b: 73)

Radcliffe is similarly keen to alert readers to another of her experiments: her transmedial use of material and narrative techniques derived from opera. She draws attention to *The Romance of the Forest*'s operatic underpinning when she refers to Peter's musical snoring which has 'more of the bass, than of any other part of the gamut in his performance' and induces a '*bravura*' response from La Motte, 'whose notes sounded discord to his ears' (Radcliffe 1986a: 59). *The Italian* refers to opera when it self-reflexively comments on its own journey from a music-filled world to one of silence and ominous sounds. Vivaldi and Paolo, on their way to the prisons of the Inquisition, travel through 'processions of musicians, monks, and mountebanks' and 'the music of serenaders, and the jokes and laughter of the revellers', eventually finding themselves in 'dark and deserted streets . . . where a melancholy and universal silence prevailed' and the quiet is interrupted only by the 'deep tone of a bell . . . rolling on the silence of the night' (Radcliffe 1986c: 194–95). Gone is the world 'where Roman ladies, in their gala habits, courtiers in their fantastic dresses, and masks of all descriptions, were hastening to the opera' (195).

Despite Emily's musings on art's inferiority to nature when her party withdraws to a late-night opera in *Udolpho*, opera is central to Radcliffe's work. It gives rise not only to certain kinds of musical scenarios, but also to new ways of signalling material about characters, their connections and their interiority. Radcliffe experiments with writing operatic scenarios as early as *A Sicilian Romance*, in which a party of banditti sing a drinking song whose 'delicacy of expression . . . appeared unattainable by men of their class' in a scene 'more like enchantment than reality' (Radcliffe 1993: 85). The opening of the novel's second volume resembles the beginning of a second act of an opera. Walking through some rocks that 'exhibited Nature in her most sublime and striking attitudes'

Madame Menon hears 'a voice of liquid and melodious sweetness ... whose melancholy expression awakened all her attention, and captivated her heart' as its 'tones swelled and died faintly away' (104–5). Rather than the voice of a 'peasant girl', this is, of course, that of Julia, the work's leading lady. In Radcliffe's next novel, the hero and heroine fall in love in a scene which is staged as opera. Singing a solo in the bosom of nature, Adeline is joined by the leading man and they duet. By the time of *Udolpho* and *The Italian*, Radcliffe's imagined worlds are not only full of sublime solos and duets performed by leading characters, but also replete with typical opera choruses – peasant girls singing arcadian rituals, singing boatmen and agricultural labourers.

It is not only in her use of musical scenarios that Radcliffe draws on opera. In operatic manner, she uses musical allusions to convey settings and provide local colour. In *Udolpho*, the gondoliers' songs reinforce the Venetian setting, while the 'Spanish Pavan' (Radcliffe 1986b: 597) heard in the Pyrenees reminds readers of both the proximity to the border and the antiquity of the world the characters inhabit. More subtly, music provides a kind of aesthetic heralding, foreshadowing change of tempo and tone and helping to lessen or build tension. Radcliffe's protagonists hear from afar the music of an arcadian idyll or a wandering war troop, an organ sounding from a church or the chants of passing pilgrims. Such music serves as a link between stages on their journeys, establishing scene changes. It also acts as a cue to the listening reader, enabling them to anticipate the adventure to come.

In *Forest* and *Udolpho*, Radcliffe experiments with a kind of musical metonymy, associating characters with particular instruments. The technique establishes correspondences between characters and forges connections across the work. In *Forest*, the correlation between the two heroines' love interests, Theodore and M. Verneuil, is intimated by the fact that both are flute-players. From the emphasis on flute-playing, an astute reader may deduce that the 'Young La Luc' who 'played the flute' is in fact Theodore (Radcliffe 1986a: 249). The lute is also used in this novel as an indicator of relationships. The association between Adeline and Clara is strengthened by the fact that the former listens to the playing of the latter 'and would often soothe her mind by attempting to repeat the airs she heard' (260). Adeline is linked to Mme Amand in a performance which reminds M. Amand of his dead wife: '"The lute", he resumed, was her favourite instrument, and when you touched it with such melancholy expression, I saw her very image before me' (286). The instrument is the means of bringing characters together, of suggesting the depths of Amand's attachment and of comparing Adeline's ability to suffer with his. It also establishes resemblances: the careful reader will not be surprised to find that Adeline and Mme Amand are related. In like manner, the oboe in *Udolpho* is metonymically associated with Emily's father, St

Aubert. Identified with him from early in the novel, its 'tender accents' suggest his paternal care and recall him forcefully after his death (Radcliffe, 1986b: 7). At the home of La Voisin, whose simple virtues were appreciated by St Aubert, the grieving Emily hears 'a pipe, that, in tone, resembled an oboe' (90). The 'pipe', a more primitive form of the oboe, references St Aubert (at the same time keeping intact the class difference) and helps to console Emily by associating him with the pastoral setting. Such is the association of the oboe with St Aubert that when, towards the end of the novel, Emily hears an oboe in the distance and weeps, the reader is supposed to know why (623).

The operatic device of 'Erinnerungsmotiv' or 'reminiscence motif', described in *The New Grove Dictionary of Opera* as a 'theme, or other coherent musical idea, which returns more or less unaltered, as identification for the audience or to signify recollection of the past by a dramatic character . . . an important ancestor of the Leitmotif,' becomes increasingly important in Radcliffe's work (Sadie 1997: III, 1288). Towards the end of *Forest*, a terrified Adeline running 'through a wild and lonely wood' hears the music of a flute (Radcliffe 1986a: 299). She recognises both 'the tone of that instrument, and the melody of that well-known air, she had heard a few preceding evenings from the shores of Provence' and has 'no doubt that it was the flute of M. Verneuil' (299, 230). Verneuil's flute-playing is not only a means of identification, it also provides a moment of connectedness which succeeds in soothing the heroine and communicating to the reader that she is ultimately safe. *Forest* and *Udolpho* are full of such recurring musical motifs, reprises that sometimes work to recall those who are absent or to evoke dual temporality, conflicted interiority or memory. In the first volume of *Udolpho*, Emily hears 'the gay melody of the dance, which she had so often listened to, as she walked with St. Aubert, on the margin of the Garonne' (Radcliffe 1986b: 93). The music is a catalyst for the release of her grief, all the more poignant because the tune itself is a happy one. Likewise, when Emily is performing in a gondola one night in Venice, the 'well-known melody brought so forcibly to her fancy the scenes and the persons, among which she had often heard it, that her spirits were overcome' (185).

Radcliffe is particularly interested in reprise that takes place in altered circumstances. It occurs at some of the most dramatic plot moments and is frequently associated with pathos. At a sublimely operatic moment in *Forest*, Theodore – awaiting death in his prison cell – recalls 'a little song which in other circumstances he had formerly sung' to Adeline, reprising it to the accompaniment of his lute. Earlier in the novel, La Motte enters Adeline's chamber only to hear her 'gently breathe, and soon after sigh' and then 'sing in her sleep' 'a melancholy little air' from 'happier days' in a 'low and mournful accent' (Radcliffe 1986a: 23). It ultimately prevents him from attempting her murder.

The Italian

The Italian, a novel filled with song, where 'vine-dressers' are 'frequently heard in trio' (37), is the most operatic of Radcliffe's works. Radcliffe is at pains to situate the main characters as singers. Ellena's voice is remarkable for its 'sweetness and fine expression' and is throughout associated with religious song (5). The quality of her 'touching and well-known' tones, distinguished amidst a general chorus, becomes the means of finding her though veiled and concealed in a convent (119). Vivaldi is 'a fine tenor' (17). Both the hero and the heroine are supported by secondary voices: Vivaldi by his friend Bonarmo in the serenade to the heroine and Ellena by her mother-substitute, Olivia. *The Italian* is very specific about who sings with whom, what they sing and in which combinations. There are many occasions, for example, when the female principals sing with, but are distinguished from, the chorus.

The Italian is more precise than its predecessors about the structure of individual numbers and the connections between numbers. Reprise occurs early in the work when Ellena sings the primary theme established in the church of San Lorenzo. She is associated with the melody to such an extent that when Vivaldi hears it again, he inexorably moves towards her (11). Later, Ellena takes up a tune associated with Vivaldi, singing 'the first stanza of the very air, with which he had opened the serenade on a former night' (27). Her rendition is prefaced by what seems to be a soliloquy, though we could also think of it as a recitative: 'Why this unreasonable pride of birth!. A visionary prejudice destroys our peace' (26). Vivaldi, onstage but invisible, is 'immoveable . . . entranced' though 'recalled' to his senses by hearing the air sung 'with such sweet pathos as the composer must have felt when he was inspired with the idea' (27). The solo soon becomes a love duet when Vivaldi, 'overcome by the temptation of such an opportunity for expressing his passion, suddenly struck the chords of the lute', and sings the second verse (27). Ellena's fainting, however, ensures that they do not sing at the same time.

Whole passages of *The Italian* are conceptualised as operatic sequences. An early example is Vivaldi's evening journey to Ellena's villa, which takes place within a landscape depicted primarily through acoustic references. Vivaldi travels through a 'stillness . . . rather soothed than interrupted by the gentle dashing of the waters of the bay below' (10). The 'hollow murmurs of Vesuvius' return 'like distant thunder' and are followed by 'pauses of silence' (10, 11, 11). Eventually, over the sounds of 'the waves and the groans of the far-off mountain', 'a chaunting of deep voices swelled from a distance', which fade away after a while (11). The sounds of the waves, groans and murmurs serve as an instrumental foundation, the preparation for the musical entrance of the choristers, whose chant is thematically linked to the opening number, sung by Ellena amidst the congregation in the opening scene. The final element in the sequence is Ellena's solo.

The Italian starts and finishes as opera. Its final scene with its feasting and dancing is, like the end of *The Romance of the Forest*, cast in the form of an opera buffa finale. Dominated musically by Paolo, it also features Vivaldi, Ellena and a chorus of peasants and retainers. There is a trio at one point, when Paolo converses with the two principals, which is followed by the refrain taken up by 'the whole company' (Radcliffe 1986c: 414). Then the principals depart (as if to prepare for a curtain call) 'amidst a choral shout' while 'all the woods and strands of Naples re-echoed with – "*O! giorno felice! O! giorno felice!*"' (414). Paolo utters some joyous nonsensical words to liberty, corrected at one point by a member of the chorus, after which, as the novel's final sentence tells us: '"*O! giorno felice!*" was again shouted in chorus by his joyful companions' (415).

Radcliffe and Opera Buffa

Radcliffe's novels of the 1790s employ a series of musical situations derived from opera (final choruses, peasant girls dancing, choruses of hunters and banditti, lovers' serenades, the songs of sailors, love arias, love duets). They appealed to their original readers' shared experience of the stage, entrusting them to know how particular numbers might sound, where they might be set, and what kind of numbers are sung by what manner of character.

Spotting references to musical situations derived from the eighteenth-century stage can alert twenty-first-century readers to atmosphere, tone and proxemics and contribute to our understanding of inter-relations and characterisation within the novels. Arguably the song of Morano in *Udolpho* provides a guarantee that this would-be rapist is capable of redemption. Certainly, it was considered worthy of being set to music by both John Percy and John Clarke-Whitfield. Knowing that the final scene of *The Italian* is an operatic finale means that we don't read Paolo, with his constant repetition of 'O! giorno felice!', as featherbrained. Realising that Theodore sings whilst in gaol in *Forest* gives a different weight to that episode (for more on prison songs, see the following section). Having an awareness of a song as a particular kind of extended moment freighted with its own emotional significance can give us a different sense of the timbre and the tempo of the text, its associations and texture.

The phrasing used by Talfourd when he discusses Radcliffe's attendance '[a]t the Opera' places her amongst the audiences at such venues as the King's Theatre and the Pantheon. Here, Italian and French operas (both 'serious opera' and opera buffa) were performed. As Curtis Price, Judith Milhous and Robert D Hume point out, much of the serious opera at the King's Theatre was becoming more 'Gothic' in the 1780s. They write of the '*Sturm und Drang* effects' of *Giulio Sabino* (performed at the King's Theatre in 1788) with its 'harrowing episode in the subterraneous vault' but say that its 'Gothic trappings ... . were as nothing compared with the real horror depicted in the adaptation of Tarchi's *Virginia*' (King's Theatre, 1786) at the end of which the heroine is carried away from a vault to be raped (Price et al. 1995: 349, 351, 351). It is plausible that such plots provided inspiration for Lewis's *The Monk*, although his scenes of horror and violence are never associated with music. Radcliffe's novels, however, are more indebted to opera buffa, with its boat songs, arcadian numbers and love arias. Her heroines venture into pastoral worlds like that of Da Ponte and Martín y Soler's *La Cosa Rara* (King's Theatre 1789), with its choruses of hunters and female peasants who play on 'the guittar' (an instrument related to the modern guitar) and bring in 'chairs decked with flowers' (Da Ponte 1789: 101). Their sentiments are like those of Neri in Palomba and Paisiello's *Gli Schiavi per Amore* (King's Theatre 1787) who, though she is not its heroine, gives utterance to words worthy of a leading lady: 'I hope, united to my dear Bronton, to lead a happy pastoral life', whether in 'hills and meads' or 'the forest gloom'; 'with him I shall sit down by a whispering rill, and enjoy the happiness of love' (Palomba 1787: 43). Radcliffe looks to opera locations like the Venice of Casti and Paisiello's *Il Re Teodoro in Venezia* (King's Theatre 1787), with its gondoliers and boatsongs, or to Palomba and Cimarosa's *Ninetta* (King's Theatre 1790) which opens with a view over the sea. Opera buffa may even have provided inspiration for the more troubling moments in Radcliffe's work; Bertati and Bianchi's *La Villanella Rapita* (King's Theatre 1790) features a scene reminiscent of *Forest*, in which a nobleman abducts a young woman of lower birth and attempts to seduce her in a rich and tasteful lodging.

The music of Radcliffe's nuns and pilgrims, however, although given operatic treatment, is not taken from an operatic source. Until the 1790s, eighteenth-century opera avoids featuring contemporary religious figures. Rather than opera providing inspiration for the Gothic novel, content from Gothic novels influences plot and representation on the musical stage. Radcliffe's singing nuns make their way into stage adaptations such as James Boaden's *The Italian Monk* (1797). The 'midnight hymn to the virgin', heard as an off-stage boat song by Julia in *A Sicilian Romance*, provides the inspiration for the off-stage religious boat song in Coleridge's *Remorse* (Radcliffe 1993: 58). As Aubrey S. Garlington points out, Gothic texts influenced 'a number of operas by French, German, and Italian composers ... Romani's libretto for Bellini's *Il pirata* (1827) was based on *Bertram* by Charles Maturin. The libretto for Rossini's *Elisabetta, Regina d'Inghilterra* (1815) was taken from a French melodrama that had been an adaptation of Sophia Lee's *The Recess*' and

'Scribe's Libretto for Gounod's *La nonne sanglante* was drawn from the "Bleeding Nun" episode in Lewis's *The Monk*' (Garlington 1962: 63).

Hearing Radcliffe

Frits Noske asserts that 'the Gothic novelist had no model for his [*sic*] enchanting melodies and harmonies' (Noske 1981: 175). I believe, however, that Radcliffe did have musical models and that some contemporary composers did succeed in realising Radcliffean music. In what follows I suggest some ways in which we might go about trying to hear the music of her novels.

Figure 6 'Giovanni Paisiello', by Elisabeth Louise Vigée Le Brun, 1791. Courtesy of Getty Images.

Paisiello (Figure 6) is a particularly promising place to look for the music of Radcliffe's novels. His operas were regularly performed at the King's Theatre and his name crops up repeatedly on concert programmes and in relation to Gothic drama. Work by Paisiello was selected, for example, by Miss Monck for Francis North's *The Kentish Barons* (1791), by William Shield for William Pearce's *The Midnight Wanderers* (1793) and *Netley Abbey* (1794) and by Stephen Storace for his and James Cobb's *The Haunted Tower* (1789). Radcliffe namechecks Paisiello herself, in a passage in her travel journals. In Belvedere House, in June 1805, she sees 'a most exquisite' painting by Claude' which she subsequently describes in a prose like that of *Udolpho*. In a near-synaesthetic experience, the landscape 'almost' conjures up Paisiello:

> The sight of this picture imparted much of the luxurious repose and satisfaction, which we derive from contemplating the finest scenes of Nature. Here was the poet, as well as the painter, touching the imagination, and making you see more than the picture contained. You saw the real light of the sun, you breathed the air of the country, you felt all the circumstances of a luxurious climate on the most serene and beautiful landscape; and, the mind being thus softened, you almost fancied you heard Italian music on the air – the music of Paisiello. (Radcliffe 1826: I, 65)

Paisiello is the sound of Radcliffe's landscapes.

The music selected and composed by Samuel Arnold for John O'Keeffe's *The Castle of Andalusia* (Figures 7 and 8), is another potential source for Radcliffean music. The work is a comic opera which first appeared (in rewritten form, after a flop the previous year) in 1782. A runaway success, it ultimately proved to be one of the most popular pieces of the day, performed, as Robert Hoskins notes, 'every year (and several times most years)' for the rest of the century (Arnold 1991: xii). *The Castle of Andalusia*, which contained selections from Handel (one of Radcliffe's favourite composers), is full of the kinds of songs that can be found in Radcliffe's novels. It has banditti singing about freedom and drink, love songs, and a joyous finale that celebrates 'social powers' (O'Keeffe 1783: 60). It is to *The Castle of Andalusia* that we can look for *A Sicilian Romance*'s singing banditti. (We can also find examples of a celebratory finale and love arias, though we can look to other works for these too).

The Castle of Andalusia's influence on Radcliffe extends further than providing examples of singing banditti. The work was a daring and successful experiment that, ultimately, provided a template for a new kind of literary Gothic. Alongside such traditional comic opera elements as multiple love plots, mistaken identities and resourceful servants pulling off outrageous disguises, O'Keeffe, described by Hazlitt as the 'English Molière' (though he was Irish), imported Gothic material into a comic opera format (Hazlitt 1899: 230). A tyrannical though weak-willed

Figure 7 Title-page from the vocal score of O'Keeffe and Arnold's
Castle of Andalusia.
The Bodleian Libraries, University of Oxford, Mus. Voc. I, 99 (8).

father teams up with his wife, an evil stepmother, to promote her daughter at the expense of his own, Victoria, 'the innocent victim of injustice and oppression', whom he attempts to force into a convent (O'Keeffe 1783: 37). His son, Don Caesar is a bandit who has imprisoned the love-sick Alphonso. As Hoskins notes, much of the content – a 'castle, the forest, the cave-in-rock, the bandits, mistaken identities and sudden recognitions' – was 'soon to become part of the stock-in-trade of the Romantic movement and its poetry', but at this moment of time and in this format it was a 'novelty' (Arnold 1991: xii). *The Castle of Andalusia*'s fusion of comic opera and Gothic literature is the first example of musicalised Gothic and it doubtless acted as a catalyst for Radcliffe's own musical experimentation. O'Keeffe and Arnold brought the Gothic novel into the comic opera: Radcliffe brought the comic opera into the Gothic novel.

Finally, I believe that the music of contemporary dramatic adaptations can (with some provisos) also furnish us with examples of what to eighteenth-century audiences passed as acceptable renditions of the imagined music of the Radcliffe's novels. Neither late eighteenth-century audiences nor Radcliffe herself was particularly concerned with historical accuracy (the flute, cello and piano in the late sixteenth-century Sicily of *Sicilian Romance* tell us as

Figure 8 Nancy Storace as Lorenza and John Fawcett as Pedrillo
in O'Keeffe and Arnold's *The Castle of Andalusia*.
Courtesy of Wikimedia Commons.

much). However, if we are looking for music that is historically accurate, that of Arnold for Boaden's adaptation of *The Italian*, set in the eighteenth century, would be a good place to start (even though *The Italian Monk*, which played at the Little Theatre in the Haymarket, is generically distinct from the opera buffa as performed at the King's Theatre). The following section offers his very credible piece for a chorus of nuns (Audio 2).

4 'Jolly Friars Tippled Here': Gothic Drama as Comic Opera

When Radcliffean Gothic hit maximum popularity in the mid-1790s, the theatres wanted their piece of the action. Radcliffe's novels spawned adaptations including Miles Peter Andrews' *The Mysteries of the Castle* and Henry Siddons' *The Sicilian Romance* (1794) both produced at Covent Garden and loosely based on *The Mysteries of Udolpho* and *A Sicilian Romance* respectively. James Boaden's *The Italian Monk* drew on Radcliffe's *The Italian*, though its title undoubtedly had Lewis fans in mind too. Adaptations of other Gothic novels also found their way onto the London stage. George Colman's *The Iron Chest* (1796) is an adaptation of William Godwin's *Things as They Are or The Adventures of Caleb Williams* (1794). Boaden's *Aurelio and Miranda*, which received its first production at Drury Lane in 1798, is derived from Lewis's *The Monk*. *The Monk* also inspired, among other productions, Charles Farley's 'New Grand Ballet Pantomime of Action' *Raymond and Agnes* (1797) with music by William Reeve (Farley 1797: Title-page). Unsurprisingly, considering the influences of the comic opera on the original novels and the dramatic exemplar provided by the ever-popular *The Castle of Andalusia*, most theatrical adaptations are rich in solo and choral song: young heroines sing airs about pastoral life, young heroes sing love songs, peasant girls dance and banditti sing drinking numbers. (Boaden's *Fountainville Forest* (1794), an adaptation of *The Romance of the Forest* with no music, is an exception to the rule.) Frequently, the music of dramatic adaptations has ambiance and emotional tone comparable to that conjured up in similar scenes in Gothic novels. *The Italian Monk*, for example, contains a number which is inspired by a passage in Radcliffe's novel when, taking refuge in a convent, Ellena hears a 'performance' which opens 'with one of those solemn and impressive airs, which the Italian nuns know how to give with so much taste and sweetness' (Radcliffe 1986c: 129). In the novel, Ellena, under pressure from an unscrupulous abbess to take the veil, experiences a feeling of rescue 'from a sense of danger' (129) when she hears the music. The corresponding number in *The Italian Monk* is heard after the heroine has left the stage, but Arnold's music conveys the sense of sublime 'calm' as the nuns sing of 'Care at the voice of her duty subsiding/Visions of rapture subliming her rest' (Boaden 1797: 27). The version here is one that might have been performed in a domestic context or at a private concert (Audio 2). It follows the vocal score's arrangement for two female voices with keyboard accompaniment, but additionally includes violins.

Audio 2 Samuel Arnold, 'Chorus of Nuns' from James Boaden's *The Italian Monk* (1797). Arranged by Seb Gillot. Sung by Issy Bridgeman and Helena Cooke, accompanied by Seb Gillot. This audio is licensed under a CC BY-NC-ND 4.0 licence. Audio file is also available at www.cambridge.org/McEvoy

The world of the adaptations, like that of the novels, is pastoral, peopled by happy and healthy workers. In *Mysteries*, the 'Chorus of Sicilian Girls going to Market' is marked in the score as 'Sprightly' (Shield 1795: 2). The huntsmen, whose voices sit in tight arrangement, are communal, cooperative and allied to nature. Their mimicking of the horn passages suggests the echoes of the hills as well as those of fellowship. The pacific joys of virtuous labour are also depicted by William Shield's introduction and siciliano for the Sicilian Mariners on the 'placid main' who sing 'Chearly chearly join the strain' as they ply their oars (24) (Audio 3). The following arrangement is for two female voices and bass, rather than the two tenors and bass given in the vocal score. Shield notes that the number was originally 'accompanied with Horns and Clarinetts behind the Scenes' (24); here, the horn part is played by the oboe.

Audio 3 William Shield, Introduction and 'Glee, Sung by the Boatmen rowing to the Shore' from Miles Peter Andrews' *The Mysteries of the Castle* (1795). Arranged by Seb Gillot. Sung by Issy Bridgeman, Helena Cooke and Laurence Williams. This audio is licensed under a CC BY-NC-ND 4.0 licence. Audio file is also available at www.cambridge.org/McEvoy

---

As in the Gothic novel, music in the stage adaptations offers respite. In *Mysteries*, for example, the song of a friendly poacher dispels the tension at the ruined castle where Julia is imprisoned. When a dramatist wants to create suspense, as for example when the intrepid heroes of *Mysteries*, Carlos and Hilario, are creeping around, there is no music, only the tolling of a bell. Sometimes music thwarts villainy. In *The Italian Monk*, as in Radcliffe's novel, the faint '*Music low and solemn*' of a requiem interrupts and checks Schedoni's plotting with the marchioness (Boaden 1797: 33).

Notably, in these works, neither Shield nor Arnold draws on what we would think of as a Gothic sound. The music for their Gothic adaptations does not depart significantly from the palette of their earlier works, whether pastoral plays, comedies of manners or of sentiment, or village romances.

Comic Opera as a Template

Mysteries was not a particularly faithful adaptation of Radcliffe's novel. Andrews had other imperatives; he was more interested in making the content work within the pre-existing template of the highly popular English comic operas that were a regular part of the repertoire at Drury Lane, Covent Garden and the Little Theatre at the Haymarket. Such fare differed from the opera to be heard at the King's Theatre and at the Pantheon. It tended to have substantially more spoken dialogue than opera buffa, and let speech carry the story. However, like comic opera all over

Europe, its plots typically feature young lovers thwarting parental opposition, deception and confusion. The characters are from different social classes and often the music is appropriate to class, with serious numbers in a more Italianate style for the higher-class characters, and comic numbers – frequently ballads – for the quick-witted servants and peasants. Formally, English comic opera draws on the traditions of the ballad opera, with a mixture of purpose-composed and borrowed numbers. Typically, strophic song (songs whose verses were set to the same music throughout) predominates. Songs are frequently to be found at the end of scenes (as is the case with the chorus of nuns in *The Italian Monk*) and acts often start and always end with music. Finales are often 'vaudevilles', (a number in which the main characters take it in turns to sing a verse or verses and, usually, the chorus sings the refrain – as in the finale to Radcliffe's *The Italian*).

Comic opera provides the template for the greater part of the Gothic drama of the 1790s. Aubrey S. Garlington argues that before the melodrama 'due to the operatic practice of the age', Gothic literature 'was incapable of any operatic presentation save in the form of comic opera' (Garlington 1962: 51). However, the issue is larger: we can substitute the word 'dramatic' for 'operatic' in this wording. Gothic drama as tragedy is practically the only genre that doesn't fall into the mode of comic opera. Comic opera is the template for musical plays, dramatic romances, farces, dramatic tales or simply plays.

NB The dividing line between the comic opera and the musical play is neither clear nor, as Jane Girdham points out, necessarily significant, 'because both were performed in the same theatres with cast members in common, and usually on the same programmes' (Girdham 1997: 123). There are, however, some rules of thumb when it comes to identifying the differences between them. Girdham observes that in a comic opera 'music provides a structural framework and is dispersed throughout the spoken dialogue', and that the 'majority of the main dramatic roles should be played by the principal singers' (131). Thus, *The Italian Monk* would be classed as a musical play rather than a full-scale comic opera because there are fewer numbers overall, they do not advance the plot, and the principal characters do not sing. The musical interest centres on the secondary heroine, Fioresca the servant girl (sung by the incomparable Mrs Bland), and also to a lesser extent on her lover Paullo (sung by Mr Suett).

Theoretically the Gothic drama didn't need to have music, as Boaden and others who wrote non-musical plays knew. Nevertheless, the majority of writers choose to include music, not only because it enhanced the production and satisfied public taste, but also because the mould of the Gothic novel of the 1790s is closely akin to that of comic opera.

Samuel Birch's afterpiece *The Adopted Child* (1795) (written as a vehicle for the 12-year-old musical prodigy, Master Welsh), illustrates just how well Radcliffean romance maps on to the conventions of the village opera, albeit in shortened two-act form. The play has a plot like that of *Castles of Athlin and Dunbayne*, with usurpation, virtuous peasants who shelter the boy heir, and a noblewoman hiding in a wood. The composer, Thomas Attwood, embraces the pastoral elements, supplying an overture with a pastorale as its second movement, as well as a setting for a solo song about the carolling of birds. Also required were pretty songs for the lower-class heroines; a more serious number for a higher-class heroine, the disinherited Clara, sister of the adopted child, who asks 'Smiling Hope' to 'Dissipate a dungeon's gloom,/ Bid the child of sadness live'; a lovers' duet; an evening song ('Lovers dread return of day') for the boy actor; and a number referencing the sublime for the villain's second-in-command, Le Sage ('Down the rugged Mountain's steep/ Hark! the plunging Waters leap') (Birch 1799: 7, 10, 5).

The Iron Chest

The comic opera template goes a long way to explaining some of the more unexpected features of *The Iron Chest* (1796) (Figure 9), which is, in John Genest's words, 'one of those jumbles of Tragedy, Comedy, and Opera, of which Colman Jun. was so fond, and which every friend of the legitimate

Figure 9 Vocal score of *Mahmoud* and *The Iron Chest*, with a portrait of Stephen Storace.
The Bodleian Libraries, University of Oxford, Mus. 301 c.96, title page.

SᴿᴬᴬSTORACCE.

Figure 10 Portrait of Nancy Storace.
Courtesy of Getty Images.

Drama must reprobate' (Girdham 1997: 190). Colman designates the work on its title page simply as a 'play'. The vocal score calls it an opera (Figure 9). In Girdham's terms, it is a musical play replete with an overture and twelve vocal numbers. She argues that despite the overture, it is 'a play with music rather than an opera', 'because the main characters do not sing', the music is related to the subplot rather than the main plot, and there is a 'small proportion of music to dialogue overall' (191). Colman's adaptation of Godwin's *Things as They Are* is as it is because Colman has a strong sense of the genre within which he was working, the composer he is writing with, and the cast he has at his disposal. The pull of comic opera as the default mode means that Colman populates *The Iron Chest* with cheeky servant-class heroines, wily poachers, and lecherous (though ultimately worthy) old gentlemen. The scale of the characters' roles reflects the musical talents (or lack of them) of the cast Colman and his composer, Stephen Storace, were able to draw on. Storace's sister, Nancy Storace, one of the most celebrated singers of the sprightly servant girl role in all Europe was a member of the company at Drury Lane and could be counted on to perform

M.ʳ *Smith, as Orson.*
Pub. Jan.1.1823. by Halgren & C.º 20 Newgate St.

Figure 11 Richard John Smith (also known as O. Smith) as Orson the bandit
in George Colman's *The Iron Chest*, 1823.

(Figure 10). If the nature of Barbara's role is dictated by the genre, its extent
can be attributed to the availability of Nancy Storace to play her. Similarly, the
beefing up of the part of Armstrong may be attributed to the fact he would be
played by Michael Kelly, the celebrated tenor. Audiences wanted to hear, and
Stephen Storace would want to write for, Kelly, his friend of many years.

By 1796, aged 33, Stephen Storace had some phenomenal successes behind him,
including the most successful English comic opera of the last decade, *The Haunted
Tower* (1789) (libretto by James Cobb) which, Fiske notes, had eighty-four performances in its first two seasons and went on to be performed over a period of fifty years
(Fiske 1973: 501) (Figure 12). Storace's music for *The Iron Chest*, though recognisably in the same tradition as the work of Arnold and Shield, is a more ambitious piece

in many respects. As Girdham points out, Storace's work for the English stage is innovative and 'introduc[es] elements from *opera buffa* into the traditional forms of English opera' (Girdham 1997: 3). *The Iron Chest* is not dominated by strophic songs that halt the action whilst characters sing them at the end of the scene, nor is it unadventurous in the grouping of vocalists. As well as strophic songs and folk-sounding numbers, it has virtuosic numbers (primarily for Kelly and Nancy Storace), trios, quartets, quintets and a glee for four voices. Moreover, its musical numbers tend to be placed *within* rather than *after* the dramatic moment, which they explore and extend, some of them ranging through different sections, moods, time signatures and genres. The following example, sung by Judith and two male bandits, starts as a night-time watch number, changes tempo and time signature when the outlaws realise their fellow bandits are arriving, and climaxes (after the extract here) when the bandits are joined by the chorus in a carousing song full of references to liberty and the joys of wine (Audio 4) (Figure 11). Notably, Storace is happier than Shield or Armstrong to venture into a sound world associated with alerts and scares and midnight thrills; there is some interesting word painting, a fluttery motif for the owl in the flute part, and a sudden diminished 7th chord when the owl hoots.

Audio 4 Stephen Storace, Trio 'Listen listen listen' from George Colman's *The Iron Chest* (1796). Arranged by Seb Gillot. Sung by Issy Bridgeman, Helena Cooke and Laurence Williams. This audio is licensed under a CC BY-NC-ND 4.0 licence. Audio file is also available at www.cambridge.org/McEvoy

---

An Uneasy Accommodation: Gothic and Comic Opera

Gothic drama frequently contains material that twenty-first-century readers, whose conception of Gothic is overwhelmingly predicated on terror and/or horror, do not expect. This is because the template provided by comic opera is not always a good fit for what we think of as the Gothic drama. In Romantic-period Gothic drama, lovable poachers burst into song, feudal tyrants are frequently weak-willed and young women might sing of 'maidens' who 'bait their hooks, /With practis'd glances, tender looks' (Boaden 1797: 12). The seeming mismatch between tone and expectation is particularly pronounced in the comic numbers that are an integral part of comic opera. Such numbers are usually associated with stock characters such as lecherous but impotent old men, gossipy women and servants and poachers who are usually gluttons and/or skivers, most of whom are not to be found in Radcliffe's or Godwin's work, although Lewis accommodated some in *The Monk* – Leonella, for example – and was to make use of more in his Gothic plays. *The Iron Chest* has a poacher who sings a comic song; the lovable rogue in *Mysteries*, Cloddy Poacher, is given two. Laden with 'hares, partridges, etc', Cloddy sings the folk-influenced number, 'In poaching all mankind delight', 'outside of an old Castle' with 'large gates' and 'a hole in the wall, that appears to lead to a subterraneous passage' (Andrews 1795: 19) (Audio 5). Here is the first of the two verses, in C rather than Eb. The arrangement in the vocal score is sparse; a harmony line in thirds has been added to the closing instrumental section.

> **Audio 5** William Shield, 'In poaching all mankind delight' from Miles Peter Andrews' *The Mysteries of the Castle* (1795). Arranged by Seb Gillot. Sung by Laurence Williams. This audio is licensed under a CC BY-NC-ND 4.0 licence. Audio file is also available at www.cambridge.org/McEvoy

There are many other examples of what are to us anomalously comic numbers in the Gothic drama of the period. The lady's maid in *Mysteries*, Annette, has a speaking song whose misogynistic observations on widows and sixty-year-old women are unimaginable in a novel by Radcliffe (Andrews 1795: 36–37). The song of the servant girl, Clara, in Henry Siddons's *The Sicilian Romance* celebrates women's ability 'to wheedle and to cheat' (Siddons 1794: 19). Siddons's opera also features another stalwart of comic opera: the drunken, lower-class male, in this case, the butler Gerbin, who sings his big number, 'SPIRIT of this dread abyss/ Appear thou with thine ugly phiz', 'half intoxicated, with a broad Sword, and Armour put on in a ludicrous Manner' (21). (The song is a comical take on the moving moment in *The Haunted Tower* when Lord William sings 'Spirit of my sainted sire', which itself draws on Walpole's *Otranto* (Cobb 1789: 40).) Francis North's *The Kentish Barons* (1791) is also full of what, to twenty-first-century readers, can seem inappropriately comic numbers, many of which are about drink. Working in an orchard, the drunkard Gam sings of bygone days ('blythe and merry,/ I frisk'd and jump'd like uncork'd Perry') and ruminates on present woes ('Oh! how I'd weep if every tear/ Wou'd turn from water into beer') (North 1791: 4). Comic song is perhaps most at odds with attitudes we associate with the Gothic when it deals with mediaeval clergy, whose drunkenness is the subject of many a fond number sung in ecclesiastical ruins. Attwood's score for *The Adopted Child*, for example, has a song with the lyrics 'how the Monks in their day must have swigg'd it away' (Attwood 1795: 22–24) while *The Iron Chest*'s Act II finale starts with three bandits singing 'Jolly Friars tippled here' (Colman 1796: 80).

What we call 'Gothic drama' frequently has unexpected content. *Mysteries*, for example, as well as the Montoni plot, in which Julia is imprisoned in a deserted castle to pressure her into marriage, has a comic plot in which Constantia is being prevented by her father, Fractioso, from marrying the man she loves. Fractioso is always going to be easily outwitted by the characters around him: his future sons-in-law, Constantia and her maid Annette. At one point, he willingly enters, and is locked into, a box where he is forced to hear sneering comments on his character. For a modern reader, the Montoni incidents are of a different order from the rest of the play and the different kinds of content sit awkwardly together. From a twenty-first-century perspective, it seems as if Radcliffean characters have accidentally strayed into a play by Goldoni, though it is more accurate to say that a Goldoni-esque opera has temporarily been hi-jacked by a Radcliffean plot. Fundamentally, *Mysteries* is not a Gothic drama but a high-spirited comic opera into which material from a recent popular Gothic novel has been imported.

Eighteenth-century audiences and playwrights do not seem to have perceived comic opera and what we think of as 'Gothic' as irreconcilable. This is unsurprising in the light of the considerable overlap between typical comic opera and Gothic novel plots. Although their designed affects may be very different, they frequently take off from similar starting points and contain related characters. Both feature tyrannical fathers determined to force their offspring into marriage, fleeing daughters and lovers in disguise. Far from blanching at supposed inappropriateness when it comes to creating what we perceive as a hybrid, Henry Siddons notes in the Advertisement to *A Tale of Terror: An Opera* (1803) that the work was initially inspired by, and even started off as a translation of, Molière's *Dom Juan* (1665), but that he quickly started to import his own elements ('the characters of Petro, Hannibal, and Paulina, are, as far as I can answer for myself, entirely new') (Siddons 1803: 1). There is evidence to suggest that, on some occasions, efforts were made to rectify some of the tonal clashes that sometimes resulted from what might have been felt to be ill-assorted content. Jeffrey Cox, comparing the first edition of *The Kentish Barons* to the version originally submitted to the censor, notes that there are songs missing from the former and suggests that their omission 'perhaps reflect[s] performance cuts' (Cox 1992: 89, fn 9). Most, though not all, of the cuts are associated with the characters of the comic drunkard and the older working-class wife.

But Is It Gothic?

Asked to guess whether a work from 1789 called *The Haunted Tower* with a plot featuring doubling and usurpation is Gothic, a twenty-first-century reader, given such cursory information, might be tempted to reply 'yes'. At a closer glance, its Gothic credentials seem to disappear. The 'haunting' in Cobb's work is designed to provoke hilarity. Gluttonous servants who have been pilfering their master's alcohol and singing a catch about being 'wond'rous merry', as well as the usurping baron himself, are scared witless by the hidden hero, Lord William, who appears as a ghost in armour (Cobb undated: 42) (Figure 13). In this work, the usurper, who prides himself on being the 'terror of the neighbourhood', is a jumped-up peasant, fearful, incompetent, ultimately harmless and even inclined towards furtive acts of reparation, giving money secretly to someone he's unjustly imprisoned (9). His son and heir knows his proper place and wishes to be a peasant again (though

Figure 12 Title-page of vocal score for Storace and Cobb's
The Haunted Tower.
The Bodleian Libraries, University of Oxford, Harding Mus. D 160.

a wealthier one). The doubling is more Goldoni than Gothic: peasants pretend to be nobles and find themselves hopelessly out of their depth. Masters and mistresses pretend to be servants and laugh at the expense of the uncouth, waging war by etiquette ('overturn her with respect and confound her with courtesy') (23). Even the stirring storm music with which *The Haunted Tower* opens – an example of *tempesta* whose conventions include an agitated style, unexpected chords, a proliferation of chromatics, exaggerated dynamics and musical painting of thunder and lightning – cannot be claimed for a supposed Gothic impulse (Audio 6). It had been lifted by Storace from his earlier opera *Gli Equivoci* (1786), a version of Shakespeare's *The Comedy of Errors*.

> **Audio 6** Stephen Storace, storm music from *The Haunted Tower* (1789), originally composed for Storace's *Gli Equivoci* (1786). Arranged by Seb Gillot. This audio is licensed under a CC BY-NC-ND 4.0 licence. Audio file is also available at www.cambridge.org/McEvoy

The Haunted Tower, with its typical comic opera arranged marriage plot played out in a class-inflected deception plot, is *almost* totally without Gothic affect. To say it has nothing to do with the Gothic, however, would be an oversimplification. The handsome image on the cover of the score plays to the vogue for Gothic (Figure 12). As noted earlier, the haunting scene borrows from *Otranto*: a bell tolls,

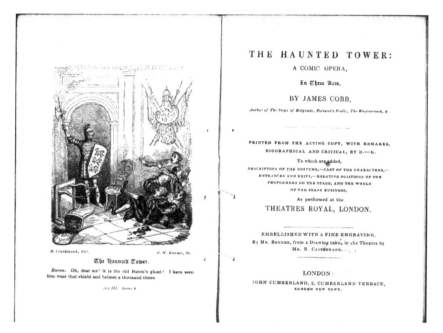

Figure 13 Frontispiece to 1832 edition of Cobb's *The Haunted Tower*.
Illustration by Cruickshank, engraved by Bonner.
Library of Congress, Music Division.

a trumpet sounds and the young hero, dressed in his father's armour, 'walks with great solemnity' across the stage (Cobb undated: 43) (Figure 13). Cobb and Storace are at the same time working within the comic opera tradition and playing to the fashion for Gothic literature. Like Radcliffe, whose first novel appeared in the same year as *The Haunted Tower*, they are beneficiaries of O'Keeffe's and Arnold's great experiment: *The Castle of Andalusia*.

The question 'is it Gothic' is not always easy to answer. Many dramatic works of the period deal with entrapment, injustice and unjust imprisonment; such subject matter had been popular in the musical theatre for decades. What were, in the twentieth century, designated 'rescue operas' (the term has now fallen out of fashion) had been popular in France since the 1760s. The most successful example, Michel-Jean Sedaine's and André Grétry's *Richard Coeur-de-lion*, had been playing in London since 1786. Whether *Richard* – a work that focuses on the comedy of village life and its light-hearted romances as much as the imprisoned king – derived inspiration from the Gothic novel is a moot point. It was, however, a significant influence on the Gothic novels of the 1790s. Its Blondel motif (in which music effects the rescue of a prisoner from a tower) occurs in numerous works (see for example *The Monk* and *Ellen Le Clair or*

The Mysterious Minstrel (1810)). In addition, *Richard* is notable for tropes found in Radcliffe and some of her successors. It has a recurring musical motif (the romance theme appears nine times) and a character associated with a musical instrument (Blondel with his violin).

The final years of the century see a boom in musical drama with usurpation, imprisonment and a love plot at the centre (some of which draw directly on Revolutionary-period French drama). John St John's 'opera in two acts' (music by Thomas Shaw) *The Island of St Marguerite* (1789), which played as the afterpiece to *The Haunted Tower*, features a character based on the man in the iron mask, who sings a great number of sad songs as he prepares to meet his doom (St John 1789: Title-page). In this work, a Temple of Liberty *literally* arises before the marriage celebration finale. John Rose's 'Musical Romance' *The Prisoner* (1792) features three pairs of lovers, rival armies, slave revolts and heroines who disguise themselves as soldiers. One of its male leads, Marcos, sings Thomas Attwood's thrilling setting of the prison song 'Despair around its horror flings/ my wish to live no longer clings' on his first appearance (Rose 1792: 15). Again, it is difficult in retrospect to say whether these texts, both of which feature conspiring nuns, are drawing on the traditions of literary Gothic as well as those of opera. Despite the imprisoned hero, malign clergy and murderous female jealousy in *The Prisoner*, the work conveys very little sense of real danger or threat. The question reversed 'do these operas influence literary Gothic?' is much easier to answer. Yes, Gothic novels of the 1790s are influenced by such 'rescue operas'.

Henry Heartwell's *The Castle of Sorrento* (Haymarket 1799), an adaptation of Duval's *Le Prisonnier* (1798), with music by Thomas Attwood, is a light-hearted work of impersonation and good-humoured roguery geared towards the delights of disguise and deception. Like *The Haunted Tower*, this 'comick opera in two acts' proves to have very little in the way of Gothic affect. A prisoner, due to be executed the following day, temporarily escapes his prison by means of a backless wardrobe. He accesses the house next door where the young heroine lives, and dines under an assumed persona with the fort's governor. However, even this light-hearted work displays considerable overlap with the Gothic novel. *The Castle of Sorrento* starts with a 'picturesque view of the country' and a heroine singing an air at sunset, then duetting with her lover (who is languishing in the castle prison) to a tune from Paisiello.

In the 1790s, many writers exploit the proximity of the literary Gothic and comic opera more knowingly. William Shield's collaborator, William Pearce, is a prime example. A decade earlier Pearce was producing work like *The Nunnery* (1785) which, though it features a lascivious aunt trying to force her niece to take the veil, presents such content in a manner very different from that of the Gothic novel. In the 1790s, however, Pearce brings the comic opera and Gothic content into a closer relation. Many of the scenarios of *The Midnight Wanderers* (1793) – stopping at an inn, perceived threat from a lower criminal class and a morning escape – and many of its characters – a young heroine Adelais, her servant, a young hero, Julian, 'MARINERS, 'BISCAYAN GIRLS, PEASANTS' – could derive from either the Gothic novel or the comic opera tradition (Pearce 1793: No page number). Its numbers include love arias, a sestetto where the heroine sings with the girls and the mariners, and even – in the original script though not in the published work – the hero's 'Address' to the absent heroine's lute (Pearce MS 1793: 39). However, *The Midnight Wanderers* consciously targets an audience of Gothic novel readers. Its second act begins with the words 'The morning-light breaks lovely over the waves' and is followed by the heroine's air 'I tread the borders of the MAIN' (Pearce 1793: 25). Adelais's name surely references a Radcliffe heroine, as do the mountainous Biscayan locale and the heroine's taste for sublime landscape. The thrilling, vocally demanding aria with which Adelais opens the first act nods to the Gothic locale, capitalising on the tension between the beautiful and the sublime. Starting with 'Long ere the tints of rosy day', it alludes to the 'varying horror round us spread', then, after modulating dramatically, settles into a pleasing siciliano (Shield 1793: 14–19). Pearce plays on the characters' confusion over which genre they occupy. Adelais is inclined to think herself the heroine of a Gothic romance. More humorously, the marquis is convinced that treachery and banditry lie all around him. Fastidious, a hypochondriac and a poltroon, he sings, 'Oh how I shake! ... I hear the ruffians mutter/ Oaths, past my skill, to utter!' The other characters respond 'No, no, 'twas but the rumbling/ Of the gale ... ' (Pearce 1793: 23–24).

Netley Abbey (1794) even more assuredly targets audiences' familiarity with the Gothic novel. The 'operatic farce in two Acts', with its two higher-class heroines, and a servant-class heroine who appears dressed as a sailor, is a knowing pastiche of sensibility, popular romances and current fashions in landscape gardening. At the opening of the work, Lucy, confronted with her father's intention to destroy woodland and a cottage in order to get a view of the picturesque Netley Abbey, asks 'And is the sweet embowered Cottage ... where I used to read the 'Dear Recess' indeed to come down?' (Pearce 1794: 1). (The original script references *The Romance of the Forest* (Pearce MS 1794: 1). Her father blames 'silly romances' for 'her absurd notions' (Pearce 1794: 2). (In the second act of the original text he references Goethe: 'But how wrong to suppose my distresses would hurt her/ Who takes such delight in 'The Sorrows of Werter' (Pearce MS 1794: 39).) Despite its gentle satire of the romance reader, the work has a suitably Gothic dénouement. Its final scene takes place in a ruined abbey where stolen goods are found, and Mr Rapine's dastardly deeds, including his usurpation of Ellen's family's property, are uncovered.

Spectacles and Operatic Romances

At the turn of the nineteenth century, Gothic content was thriving in London's theatre scene. Tragedies and poetic dramas, such as Joanna Baillie's *De Monfort* (1800), held their own in the legitimate playhouses. At both the older playhouses and the newer 'illegitimate' venues there was a range of fare: melodrama (the subject of the final section), Gothic pantomimes and ballets and, particularly in the illegitimate venues (those legally prohibited from offering spoken word drama), 'spectacles'.

If the newer venues found inventive ways of circumventing the restrictions placed upon them, their inventiveness didn't always extend to musical innovation. In the period before melodrama bursts on the scene (and frequently afterwards), even works with very horrid titles still contain music recognisably in the same idioms as those found in the legitimate playhouses. Such is the case with 'The Cottage of Peace' ('The Poetry by Mr. Upton') from the 'New Grand Caledonian Spectacle' *The Iron Tower* (1801) which played at Astley's Amphitheatre (Sanderson 1801: Title-page) (Audio 7). James Sanderson's 'Pastoral Ballad 'gives the lie to those inclined to believe that there is a clear divide in style between the newer and older (or illegitimate and legitimate) venues. Here is the first of the two verses.

Audio 7 James Sanderson, first verse of 'The Cottage of Peace' from Astley's 'Grand Caledonian Spectacle Romance' *The Iron Tower or The Cell of Mystery* (1801), lyrics by Mr Upton. Arranged by Seb Gillot. Sung by Issy Bridgeman. This audio is licensed under a CC BY-NC-ND 4.0 licence. Audio file is also available at www.cambridge.org/McEvoy

---

The music for J C Cross's 'dramatic spectacle', *Julia of Louvain, or, Monkish Cruelty* (Royal Circus, 1797) also seems to have been similar to that of the patent theatres (no sheet music has yet been found). The published description of the work indicates that it included choral numbers for boatmen and for villagers working on the vintage, a song for a foppish French servant, and a 'PATHETIC BALLAD' sung by a nun (Cox 1992: 144). Musically speaking, the only notable difference between *Julia* and the Gothic drama as comic opera that played at the legitimate theatres is that in *Julia*, the villainous antagonist sings. This is unsurprising given that legally he was not permitted to speak. St Pierre, about to compel the heroine to marry him or be killed, sings what was probably an *aria di tempesta*. The description notes that it is a 'bravura' number that starts 'The tempest rages here! in vain/ I bid the storm depart' (145).

The second decade of the new century sees the rise of the 'operatic romance', examples of which include Lewis's *One O'Clock or The Knight and the Wood-Daemon* (1811) (variously described as a 'dramatic romance' a 'musical romance' and a 'grand Romantic opera') and Samuel James Arnold's *The*

Devil's Bridge (1812), both of which were produced at the Lyceum (known between 1816 and 1818 as the English Opera House). The Lyceum specialised in the operatic romance. It was managed by Samuel James Arnold, the son of the composer Samuel Arnold. A prolific playwright and librettist, S. J. Arnold's works tend to be overlooked today not least because most of his play texts were unpublished, though the vocal scores frequently appeared in splendid editions. William Hazlitt was scathing when it came to S. J. Arnold's literary ability, noting in a review in 1815 that he 'may be safely placed at the head of a very prevailing class of poets. He writes with the fewest ideas possible; his meaning is more nicely balanced between sense and nonsense, than that of any of his competitors; he succeeds from the perfect insignificance of his pretensions, and fails to offend through downright imbecility' (Hazlitt 1821: 148). Even Hazlitt, however, had to admit that S. J. Arnold knew his business: 'His characters are the shadows of a shade; but he keeps a very exact inventory of his scenery and dresses, and can always command the orchestra' (148). In fact, S. J. Arnold was a stunningly good fit for the job. From a musical background, he had written and composed his own musical drama *Foul Deeds Will Rise* (1804) and provided the libretto for his father's *The Shipwreck* (1796). He had also trained as an artist and was a published novelist (although, despite the title, *The Creole, or, the Haunted Island* (1796), is more *Rasselas* than Radcliffe).

In 1810, S. J. Arnold collaborated with Henry Bishop on a 'serio comic opera', *The Maniac or The Swiss Banditti*. Later in the decade, the work would probably have been described as an 'operatic romance', containing very similar content, range of numbers and tone. *The Maniac* has the familiar blend of light-hearted comedy, double plotting and three sets of lovers. Here is Bishop's touching and fragmentary 'Love is the Essence of a part', sung by the work's gently mad heroine, Lauretta, whose heart and sanity are lost to a soldier (Audio 8).

Audio 8 Henry Bishop, 'Love is the Essence of a part' from Samuel James Arnold's *The Maniac or The Swiss Banditti* (1810). Sung by Issy Bridgeman. This audio is licensed under a CC BY-NC-ND 4.0 licence. Audio file is also available at www.cambridge.org/McEvoy

---

Works such as *The Maniac* and the numerous operatic romances of the early nineteenth century are successors of the 1790s comic opera, in which song is central and music is associated with individual and communal expression. 'Romance' as a term applied to Gothic drama had of course been circulating for a while; Rose's *The Prisoner* (1792) was presented as 'musical romance' and Lewis's *Adelmorn* (1801) as a 'romantic drama'. The term, however, conveys extra meanings after the arrival of the melodrama. In Arnold's hands, it signals continuities with the comic opera and points to a world of abundant song where the music is not meant to terrify. It promises the plotting and ambiance of comic opera, and, to quote Hazlitt again, the 'apparitions of gilded sceptres, painted groves and castles, wandering damsels, cruel fathers and tender lovers' (148).

The Gothic operatic romance is comic opera deluxe. It positively bursts with numbers, most of which are drawn from a Radcliffean sound world. S. J. Arnold's *The Devil's Bridge* (1812), for example, begins with an echo quartet, has hunting horns sounding in the distance and features storms. There is music for the heroine, the faithful hero, secondary characters, choruses of peasants, soldiers and huntsmen – but not for the villain. It is brimful of updated versions of the kinds of songs found in a 1790s comic opera: love arias, a 'Chorus of Chasseurs' who sing 'On to the Chase' (Horn and Braham undated: 45–51), soldiers who sing 'Away to the Dungeon . . . resistance is vain' (66–9), a recognition song, a bravura number for the leading lady, Rosalvina, when, like a Radcliffe heroine, she sings 'Bright sun I adore thee when rising sublime' (52–8), a 'Hush! Hush cautious Step' number (32–5), a touching two tenors moment ('Rest Weary Traveller') (76–80), and various evening numbers, such as the following, the tender but perky 'Hark it is the vesper bell' by Charles Horn who, with John Braham, was jointly responsible for the music of the production (7–11) (Audio 9).

> **Audio 9** Charles Horn, 'The Vesper Bell, a Quartetto' from Samuel James Arnold's *The Devil's Bridge* (1812). Arranged by Seb Gillot. Sung by Issy Bridgeman, Helena Cooke, Guy Cutting and Laurence Williams. This audio is licensed under a CC BY-NC-ND 4.0 licence. Audio file is also available at www.cambridge.org/McEvoy

The Devil's Bridge also contains a 'celebrated Prison Song, Sung by Mr Braham, with universal applause' (Horn and Braham undated: 70–75) (Audio 10). Braham, like Michael Kelly, was a star tenor who went on to compose (Figure 2). His prison song for Count Belino is a substantial number that takes us through various aspects of the hero and his situation. The opening passage suggests the stern reality of imprisonment which the hero faces with stoicism. There is some nice word painting with an echo motif and the stop at the word 'silence' (71). The second section, the canzonetta, reveals the hero's sensibility, his tenderness and sense of loss. In the last section, the hero hopes, looking forward to liberty, love and hunting.

> **Audio 10** John Braham, 'The Prison Song' from Samuel James Arnold's *The Devil's Bridge* (1812). Arranged by Seb Gillot. Sung by Guy Cutting. This audio is licensed under a CC BY-NC-ND 4.0 licence. Audio file is also available at www.cambridge.org/McEvoy

Conclusions

Approaching Gothic drama through its music is a useful exercise. It encourages us to think about generic alliances and reminds us that, as a generic designation, 'Gothic' is an anachronistic term. For eighteenth-century audiences, there is no such thing as Gothic drama. The kind of content associated with what we term Gothic drama (imprisonment, injustice, generational conflict) is shared with other genres. While we expect such content to cause particular affects, such expectation is not necessarily shared by eighteenth-century audiences, writers and composers. What we choose to call the Gothic drama can overlap with other genres (most notably the comic opera) to such an extent that the affectivity we habitually associate with Gothic is not to be found. For much, perhaps most, 'Gothic drama' of the period, the term Gothic is insufficient and our models of genre are inadequate. The description 'comic Gothic' is not particularly helpful.

Garlington argues that melodrama provides the first satisfactory 'musical treatment' for Gothic literature and asserts that 'the older concept of English opera' was incapable of supplying adequate music for the 'new literature' (Garlington 1962: 63, 51). He is undeniably right when it comes to examining melodrama's aptness for conveying certain kinds of Gothic affect. He is, however, on shakier ground when he writes about the comic opera. The comic opera does not fail to provide the correct affects for the 1790s Gothic novel. Garlington is looking from the wrong direction. Convinced of the appropriateness of the musical idioms associated with melodrama for expressing the affects he associates with the Gothic, he does not consider that the writers of the comic operas were not aiming to convey (or inspire) terror, suspense, fear or unease. Far from it: they wanted music to convey love, tender melancholy, comedy, the joys of the working life and the pastoral world. Moreover, Garlington fails to realise that the Gothic novels of the 1790s do not, for the most part, associate the new affects they bring into being with disturbing music. For playwrights and composers in the 1790s, suspense might be preceded by a bell, but it comes without music. The main exception to the general rule that the music of the 1790s romance is not disturbing is the music of the (real or supposed) supernatural, for example, Laurentini's singing in *Udolpho* or the devilish music of *The Monk*. Notably, however, such music is most frequently described as 'sweet', something which most melodramatic music conspicuously isn't.

In the previous section, I suggested, in relation to Radcliffe, that the music of dramatic adaptations has the potential to bring us closer to the music of her novels. The principle can be more widely applied. The music not only of adaptations but also of other Gothic drama can enrich our understanding of other Gothic novels of the period too (which is not surprising, as the dramatic works are drawing directly on the comic operas that inspired Gothic romances). The claim evidently needs to be hedged round with provisos. Sometimes, as we have seen, the requirements for

English comic operas differ spectacularly from those for the Gothic novel. In some cases, the adaptation is not really an adaptation, but a work into which, to quote from the prologue to *Mysteries*, a mere 'dash of terror' has been introduced (Andrews 1795: Prologue). Some numbers signally do not correspond with those in the Gothic novels. Michael Kelly's 'Celebrated Gypsey Song of Cross my Hand & you shall know' in Boaden's *Aurelio and Miranda* (1798) does not suggest the 'folly and delirium' associated with the dance of the gypsy in *The Monk* (Lewis 1995: 35) (Audio 11). In the composer's defence, however, it should be noted that he was composing for a thoroughly sanitised version of *The Monk*, devoid of the supernatural, with a very public-spirited gypsy. Lewis's verdict on Boaden's play was 'so bad ... so bad!' (Boaden 1980: xl). Here is the first of the song's three verses; the high soprano notes at the very end are taken from the third verse arrangement.

Audio 11 Michael Kelly, 'The Celebrated Gypsey Song of Cross my Hand & you shall know' from James Boaden's *Aurelio and Miranda* (1798). Arranged by Seb Gillot. Soloist Issy Bridgeman, with Helena Cooke, Guy Cutting and Laurence Williams. This audio is licensed under a CC BY-NC-ND 4.0 licence. Audio file is also available at www.cambridge.org/McEvoy

---

Despite these provisos, hearing the music of hunters, of prisoners, of peasant girls, of boatmen and banditti, of heroines celebrating the pastoral or going picturesquely mad in comic operas, musical plays and operatic romances can provide a useful route into the sound world of the 1790s romance, though not necessarily, as we shall see, into the sound worlds of later novels. The prison songs sung by the heroes of the drama of the early 1980s and 1990s can contribute to our understanding of Theodore in *The Romance of the Forest*, or Du Pont in *Udolpho* and help us to see what Lewis is sending up in *The Castle Spectre*. Such songs typically start with sombre reflection, pass through reminiscence and progress to hope. The hero of *The Island of St Marguerite* starts by lamenting 'From dreary dreams I wake to woe' but finishes by hymning 'hope sweet hope' that 'delights to cheer the Prison gloom and here e'en here forbids forbids despair' (Shaw c. 1789: 26–7).[4] Likewise, the chorus of huntsmen in *Mysteries*, with its full horn parts and echo effects, can help us envisage Valancourt in his sonic world – or indeed Percy, whose 'mellow horn' 'carol[s]' in the 'green hills' in *The Castle Spectre* (Lewis 1798: 71).

The music of Gothic drama is necessary listening for twenty-first-century readers. When we factor it in, we find that Gothic drama is more varied than what Francesca Saggini refers to as 'A Stage of Tears and Terror' (Saggini 2015: 23). Restoring the music of Gothic drama enables us to restore its tenderness, comedy, romance, merriment and even, as we shall see in the next section, its transcendence.

---

[4] See https://commons.wikimedia.org/wiki/File:Thomas_Shaw_-_The_Island_of_Saint_Marguerite_-_%27For_dreary_dreams_I_wake_to_woe%27_(1).jpg.

5 'The Captivation of an Unearthly Music': Michael Kelly, *The Castle Spectre* and *Remorse*

Matthew Lewis's *The Monk* bears the tell-tale signs of a novel that has – at least in part – been conceived as a stage work. There is a reference to a play and an audience on the first page. Music and sound effects are used to move in and out of what seem to be envisaged as theatrical scenes. Phrases reminiscent of stage directions, such as 'the music ceased' and 'the voice ceased' are frequent, as are references to pauses.

Figure 14 Michael Kelly, painted by Thomas Lawrence, engraved by John Neagle.
From The New York Public Library https://digitalcollections.nypl.org/items/
510d47 da-f7e2-a3d9-e040-e00a18064a99

Music is to be found through most of the first two volumes; the notable exception is
at the end of volume I, when ominously the banditti do not sing. The music climaxes
in the third and final volume. A long and varied number starts with a chorus of nuns
in the chapel accompanied by 'the full swell of the organ', continues with Virginia
de Villa-Franca's 'single strain of harmony', the tolling of the 'Convent-Bell' at
midnight, a chorus of monks 'chaunting Hymns', and hymns from different groups
of nuns (Lewis 1995: 345–46). The novel's subsequent lack of music and focus on
silence is an act of genre betrayal, designed to wrongfoot readers.

Lewis's play *The Castle Spectre* is not as replete with music as *The Monk*, with
only four numbers in the original production. (Dorothea Jordan decided to omit
a fifth number, written for Angela.) However, the play's success and its 'prodi-
gious run' (Kelly 1826: II, 140) were due in no small part to what Lewis described
as its 'beautiful music' (Lewis 1798: 103). The number of vocal scores surviving
in archives testifies to its popularity; the British Library has editions from four
separate publishers of the period in its collection. For his composer, Lewis turned
to Michael Kelly. Stephen Storace, who had been desperately ill during the
rehearsals for *The Iron Chest*, had died within a week of its opening.

Kelly was an Irish tenor (Figure 14). After a highly successful stage debut in
Dublin in his teens, he had been sent to study in Italy, where he met Nancy and
Stephen Storace. By 1784, all three had moved to Vienna, where Nancy and Kelly
were contracted to the Burgtheater and featured in the first production of *The
Marriage of Figaro* (1786). Nancy sang Susanna; Kelly played the roles of Basilio
and Don Curzio. In 1787, they all left Vienna for London. Kelly became principal
tenor at Drury Lane, remaining so till 1808 and, from 1789, also regularly sang at
the Ancient Music Concerts, the King's Theatre and Covent Garden. Eventually he
was to become musical director and house composer at Drury Lane. He was well
fitted for this position by a wealth of experience from opera houses throughout Italy
and in Vienna, and an extensive repertoire, updated by trips to Paris in the early
1790s. Kelly had form when it came to Gothic drama, having played Lord William
(to his partner Anna Crouch's Lady Elinor) in *The Haunted Tower* and Armstrong
in *The Iron Chest*; he had also been the imprisoned male lead in *The Prisoner* and
The Isle of St Marguerite, and played Richard in *Richard the Lionheart* in more
than one production. Kelly was a sociable and well-liked figure who, had 'the rare
talent of acquiring and preserving the good opinion of every man with whom he
became acquainted: not by sycophancy, but by cordiality of manners, a heartiness,
a warmth, which convinced you that to render you a service was a pleasure done to
himself' (Anonymous 1827: 61). He and Lewis got on famously. Their collabor-
ations include *Adelmorn the Outlaw* (1801), *The Wood Daemon* (1807) and *Venoni*
(1808). Ultimately Kelly was to provide music for some highly significant Gothic
productions, including Samuel Taylor Coleridge's *Remorse* (1813) and Joanna
Baillie's *De Monfort* (1800) (for which unfortunately no music seems to survive).

The Castle Spectre

Kelly was proud of *The Castle Spectre*'s first number, 'Megen-oh! Oh! Megen-Ee!' (Audio 12). Years later, he recalled bursting out with it joyfully on the ferry passing Conwy Castle, scene of the play's action, much to the surprise of the boatmen and fellow passengers (Kelly 1826: II, 312–13). 'Megen' is a glee – a part-song associated with conviviality, commonly understood as deriving from the 'ancient' traditions of British vocal music. Glees frequently form part of comic operas. *Mysteries* has glees for the Sicilian mariners and the sportsmen; *The Iron Chest* opens with a glee for four voices. Traditionally glees were unaccompanied and performed by male singers; however, at this period it had become increasingly common for women to sing in them too.

The scene in which 'Megen' is sung is a facetious take on the Blondel scenario. A rescue number sung by quick-thinking, loyal servants outside the tower where the young hero, Percy, is imprisoned, 'Megen' is the means of effecting his liberation. Typically for Lewis, the song is both satirical and self-reflexive. As in *Adelmorn the Outlaw* (1801) with its relentless musical puns, Lewis uses the musical moment to step outside the frame and provide some humorous reflections on the mise-en-scène. The faux mediaeval words comically put Percy in the position of 'Fair Emma' the 'Lady Bright', about to jump into her lover's arms into the boat that will bear them both away (Lewis 1798: 39, 38). The split action, which alternately

Figure 15 First page of Michael Kelly's ghost music for *The Castle Spectre*. The Bodleian Libraries, University of Oxford, Mus. Voc. I, 103 (3), p. 6.

focuses on the three separate parties (prisoner, gaolers, rescue party), is juxtaposed with the tight co-ordination of the three parts of the song, while the sleek statement-refrain structure contrasts with the urgency of the life and death negotiations going on within the tower. 'Megen' is a light-hearted number in a bouncy 3/8. There is nothing urgent about it, as underlined by the continued repetition with alterations of its final cadence. Here is the first of the number's three verses.

> **Audio 12** Michael Kelly, first verse of 'Megan oh oh Megan ee' from Matthew Lewis's *The Castle Spectre* (1798). Sung by Guy Cutting, Laurence Williams and Helena Cooke. This audio is licensed under a CC BY-NC-ND 4.0 licence. Audio file is also available at www.cambridge.org/McEvoy

Unlike any of the works discussed until this point, *The Castle Spectre* featured a 'real' ghost, despite the fact that, as Lewis notes, managers and actors 'all combined to persecute my *Spectre*, and requested me to confine my Ghost to the Green-Room' (Lewis 1798: 102–103). In Act IV Scene ii, the ghost of Evelina, the heroine's mother, after the striking of a bell, sings Lewis's lullaby from behind the scenes (Audio 13) (Figure 15). It is short and sweet, in a major key, clear and simple, and was accompanied originally by an instrument popular with ladies in the late eighteenth century: the guittar. This version has a keyboard.

> **Audio 13** Michael Kelly and Matthew Lewis, 'The Spectre Song' from Matthew Lewis's *The Castle Spectre* (1798). Sung by Issy Bridgeman, accompanied by Seb Gillot. This audio is licensed under a CC BY-NC-ND 4.0 licence. Audio file is also available at www.cambridge.org/McEvoy

For Evelina's actual appearance, Kelly selected some existing music by the Italian composer Niccolò Jommelli (Audio 14) (Figures 15 and 16). His choice of a chaconne, a slow and stately dance that typically unfolds over a large canvas, perhaps gestures to the larger timescale Evelina's existence spans.

> **Audio 14** Michael Kelly, 'Music from the Oratory while the Ghost appears' from Matthew Lewis's *The Castle Spectre* (1798), adapted from Niccolò Jommelli. Arranged by Seb Gillot. This audio is licensed under a CC BY-NC-ND 4.0 licence. Audio file is also available at www.cambridge.org/McEvoy

When the 'music ceases', Angela shrieks 'Stay, lovely spirit! – Oh! stay yet one moment!' but the 'Spectre waves her hand, as bidding her farewell. Instantly the organ's swell is heard' (Lewis 1798: 80). For this moment, closing the scene and the act, Kelly composed this short, straightforward 'Jubilate', originally performed by a 'chorus of female voices' (Lewis 1798: 80) (Audio 15) (Figure 16).

Audio 15 Michael Kelly, 'Jubilate' from Matthew Lewis's *The Castle Spectre* (1798). Arranged by Seb Gillot. Sung by Issy Bridgeman, Helena Cooke, Guy Cutting and Laurence Williams. This audio is licensed under a CC BY-NC-ND 4.0 licence. Audio file is also available at www.cambridge.org/McEvoy

---

There is no sinister music in *The Castle Spectre*. 'Megen', the show's 'favourite', which was frequently reprinted on its own is associated with relief and release from danger and is immediately followed by Percy's daring jump into the boat waiting below (Audio 12). Even the music for the spectre's appearance is not eerie (Audio 14). Instead, it is full, warm and tender.

Over a generation later, audience members still remembered the effectiveness of the music that accompanies Evelina, a '*tall female figure; her white and flowing garments spotted with blood . . . a large wound . . . upon her bosom*', as she advances across the stage (Lewis 1798: 79) (Audio 14). In his memoir of the actor John Philip Kemble (who played Percy in the production), James Boaden describes the moment as 'unearthly'. However, its unearthliness is not associated with an uncanny frisson. The music is heard with 'delight' not terror and its 'captivation' is such that it stops time for the biographer, who apologises to his subject for his detour.

> I yet bring before me, with delight, the waving form of Mrs. Powell, advancing from the suddenly illuminated chapel, and bending over Angela (Mrs. Jordan) in maternal benediction; during which slow and solemn action,

Figure 16 Second page of Michael Kelly's ghost music for *The Castle Spectre*. The Bodleian Libraries, University of Oxford, Mus. Voc. I, 103 (3), p. 7.

the band played a few bars, or rather the full *subject* at all events, of Jomelli's [*sic*] *Chaconne*, in his celebrated overture in three flats. Pardon, my dear Kemble, the captivation of an unearthly music. I will attend upon Percy and yourself immediately. (Boaden 1825: II, 206)

Remorse

The success of Kelly's music for *The Castle Spectre* made him, many years later, the obvious choice of composer for Coleridge's *Remorse*, a work which also features music in a pivotal scene associated with the supernatural. The protagonist, Alvar, having survived a plot by his brother, Osorio, to have him murdered, returns in disguise as The Stranger and stages a supernatural summoning in an attempt to make Osorio confess his guilt and provoke him to remorse. The scene, which opens the third act, is layered with music both figurative and real. Here is the graceful, fluid and soothing music accompanying the cue 'When Scene opens' (Kelly undated: 1) (Audio 16).

Audio 16 Michael Kelly, music for 'When Scene opens' from Samuel Taylor Coleridge's *Remorse* (1813). Arranged by Seb Gillot. This audio is licensed under a CC BY-NC-ND 4.0 licence. Audio file is also available at www.cambridge.org/McEvoy

---

The 'Soft music from an Instrument of Glass or Steel' – a glass harmonica or its equivalent – is not included here, as it was supposed to be improvised. Here, however, is the music depicting the sounds of departed souls that 'Girdle this round earth in a dizzy motion,/With noise too vast and constant to behold' (Coleridge 1989: 34) (Audio 17). It is a simple but effective long, drawn-out F major chord, dying away to nothing. In the absence of a glass harmonica, it has been arranged for strings and wind.

Audio 17 Michael Kelly, music for 'The rushing of your congregated wings' from Samuel Taylor Coleridge's *Remorse* (1813). Arranged by Seb Gillot. This audio is licensed under a CC BY-NC-ND 4.0 licence. Audio file is also available at www.cambridge.org/McEvoy

---

Remorse's showstopper was the music for the invocation to call the supposedly murdered man from the dead and ask God for pity on his soul (Audio 18). This 'mild spell' (Coleridge 1989: 35) was sung by the celebrated Mrs Bland, who according to Kelly, sang 'with all the refreshing purity of her unsophisticated style, and with that chaste expression and tenderness of feeling which speak at once as it were to the heart' (Kelly 1826: II, 309). If the description of Maria Theresa Bland's voice recalls that of Emily in *Udolpho*, so do Coleridge's lyrics read like a play list for a 1790s Gothic novel. Like Radcliffe's lyrics, they are full of musical and sonic references – to 'midnight breezes', a 'deep long lingering knell', and a 'cadence

[that] dies away/ On the yellow moonlight sea' (Coleridge 1989: 35–36). There is a magical transition at the end of the invocation, as the words of the song become actuality. Bland sings 'The boatmen rest their oars and say . . . Miserere Domine' – and then the chorus sings a miserere (Kelly undated: 2). Kelly notes that Coleridge had sought in vain whilst in Italy to get the miserere set satisfactorily, but that Kelly himself 'was fortunate enough to hear from the highly-talented author of the play, that my music was every thing he could have wished' (Kelly 1826: 309). The miserere is recognisably church-related, though a little off-kilter – particularly with those insistent triplets on the word 'domine' in the exposed bass part. Feasibly, the fact that Kelly, though Catholic, did not, unlike the Italian composers addressed by Coleridge, write in a convincing Catholic liturgical idiom may have made his music more acceptable to the writer. For the characters onstage, the 'miserere' becomes a moment of communal devotion that doesn't sound too Catholic.

Kelly's music for *Remorse*'s 'mild spell' has a family resemblance to that for the ghost's appearance in *The Castle Spectre*. Both pieces are serene, and their iteration marks a moment of blessed relief, a respite from the turmoil, machinations and madness that characterise the rest of the plot. They operate within earlier eighteenth-century conventions of what has since been called 'ombra', music associated with the supernatural. Ombra has many modes. In these instances Kelly is drawing on the type in which the sublime is evoked through stately dignity, tempi are slow, phrasing expansive, and the use of wind instruments common (Audio 18 and Audio 14). As with the Jommelli chaconne in *The Castle Spectre*, the invocation is played at a moment when everything is brought to a stop (Audio 14 and Audio 18). Notably the source of the sound is obscured: Mrs Bland is offstage. The audience is compelled to listen and adapt to a different tempo.

Audio 18 Michael Kelly, 'Hear, sweet Spirit' and 'Miserere' from Samuel Taylor Coleridge's *Remorse* (1813). Arranged by Seb Gillot. Soloist Issy Bridgeman, with Helena Cooke and Laurence Williams. This audio is licensed under a CC BY-NC-ND 4.0 licence. Audio file is also available at www.cambridge.org/McEvoy

---

'A Thrilling Sensation Appeared to Pervade the Great Mass of Congregated Humanity'

When Kelly broke into 'Megen' on the ferry outside Conwy Castle, he did so not only because he was at the site of the play's action, but also for sheer exuberance, fond recollection and, presumably, a bit of showing off (Audio 12). We have testimony for extra-theatrical performance, associated with fresh air, energy and exuberance, for other Gothic-related music of the period too. For almost a hundred and fifty years, productions of Shakespeare's *Macbeth* (which, though not a Gothic play, is frequently referenced in Gothic texts) featured the witches singing and dancing to the following celebrated music by Richard Leveridge (Audio 19). Percy Bysshe Shelley's friend, Amos, writes of Shelley 'singing with the buoyant cheerfulness in which he often indulged, as he might be running nimbly up and down stairs, the Witches' songs in Macbeth' ([Amos. A] 1848: 390). Samuel Palmer wrote that, in the 1820s, he and his fellow-artists, 'The Ancients', could be found singing the witches' music at night-time in the 'hollow clefts and deserted chalk-pits' round Shoreham in Kent (Palmer 1892: 42).

Audio 19 Richard Leveridge, 'Let's have a Dance upon the Heath' (1702), composed for Shakespeare's *Macbeth*. Soloist Issy Bridgeman, with Helena Cooke and Guy Cutting. This audio is licensed under a CC BY-NC-ND 4.0 licence. Audio file is also available at www.cambridge.org/McEvoy

---

Leveridge's exhilarating music is a salutary reminder that music associated with black magic and malevolence need not come in the idioms that we expect. It has very little in common with the music that frequently accompanies the witches' appearances on stage and film today (see, for example, the Celtic weird provided by Jed Kurzel for Justin Kurzel's *Macbeth* of 2015). Similarly, Kelly's music for *The Castle Spectre* and *Remorse* does not tally with the kinds of affects we associate with bloodied ghosts or occult dabbling (Audio 14 and Audio 18). Evelina the ghost sings, and it is a short, simple affair (Audio 13). Evelina appears and the music is tender and sublime (Audio 14). The incantation in *Remorse* is a serene piece written for the most serene singer of the age (Audio 18).

I have been arguing that listening to its music helps us to recover some of the fullness of the Gothic drama. However, in some cases exposure to the music is not enough to enable twenty-first-century readers and audiences to gauge its original affects. Sometimes, and this is certainly true in the case of the Jommelli (Audio 14), the vocal score is not sufficiently informative, being rather an aide mémoire for those who had seen the performance (or heard the music elsewhere) than an attempt to provide an accurate transcription. A vocal score was typically limited to three musical lines; as Fiske points out, 'only the skeleton got printed and none of the flesh' (Fiske 1973: 297–98). Additionally, our 'takeaway' isn't necessarily the same as that of 1790s audiences. The kind of ombra in the Jommelli, its mode of realising the sublime, is more historically specific than many others. Thus, even diligent and sensitive critics accessing Kelly's vocal score have failed to pick up on its original affect. Michael Gamer refers to it as 'dreary' (Gamer 2018: 37), while Aubrey S. Garlington declares that 'it bears no relationship to the business at hand, and the music becomes "ghostly" only by its juxtaposition to a particular scene' (Garlington 1962: 58).

Boaden's account of the audience's response to the appearance of Evelina in *The Castle Spectre* is a useful supplement to both the vocal score and Lewis's script (Audio 14). The play text describes the music's 'soft and plaintive strain' and tells us that Evelina 'seems' to bless Angela and that, following Evelina's appearance, Angela has a 'wild look' (70). However, this level of detail is not enough for us to be able to second-guess or reconstruct the affects experienced by late eighteenth-century audiences, or to escape a circle of confirmation bias, based on our experiences of texts in which seemingly similar scenes are played to evoke horror or terror. Listening to the Jommelli in conjunction with reading Boaden's description of its reception (not just within the theatre at the time of performance, but in Boaden's long memory) points us towards a reading of the end of Act IV as a moment in which, despite the bloodied apparition, horror subsides, and a rapturous calm takes its place (Figure 17).

Neither the Jommelli nor the music for the milder spell in *Remorse* was intended to conjure up unease or suspense, to scare its audience or provoke terror (Audio 14 and Audio 18). Instead, both pieces aimed at, and by all accounts succeeded in, inducing awe and wonder in their listeners. Here is Kelly's account of the audience response to *Remorse*'s incantation (Audio 18):

> The chorus of boatmen chaunting on the water under the convent walls, and the distant peal of the organ, accompanying the monks while singing within the convent chapel, seemed to overcome and soothe the audience; a thrilling sensation appeared to pervade the great mass of congregated humanity, and, during its performance, it was listened to, with undivided attention, as if the minds and hearts of all were rivetted and enthralled by the combination presented to their notice; and at the conclusion the applause was loud and protracted. (Kelly 1826: II, 309)

Although Kelly employs the word 'thrilling', the thrill is one of together-ness, associated with hearts and minds rather than nerves. The audience is mentally overpowered but also soothed. The moment is reminiscent of the Radcliffean sublime.

These musical moments in Coleridge's and Lewis's plays – when ghosts give way to divine visions, or occult threat to blessing – have equivalents in novels of the period, at moments when present danger is forestalled, or past wrongs set to right. In the novels, as in the plays, the music of the supernatural is serene and glorious, solemn and dignified, sublime and soothing. Towards the climax of *The Haunted Priory*, Alphonso, Don Isidor and the Baron dig down into the convent ruins to find the entrance to the chapel. A 'bell tolled and straight the chapel within was illuminated' (Cullen 1794: 154). Through an open door, 'a most transporting peal of musick struck up, and voices more than human sung the Nunc dimittis' (157). An even more full-blown instance of supernatural music can be found in R P M Yorke's *The Haunted Palace* (1801), in which explorers of ruins after hearing 'melting strains' from an 'angelic harmonist', which 'seemed still to vibrate upon the ear' and 'wrapt' the 'senses' in 'heavenly extacy' find themselves trapped in a ruined,

THE CASTLE SPECTRE.

Figure 17 Transparency depicting the appearance of Evelina in *The Castle Spectre*, designed by W. Orme, print made by Charles Turner, published by Edward Orme.
© The Trustees of the British Museum

music room (Yorke 1801: I, 238). (One of the characters, we are told, is 'literally enveloped in great bunches of sculptured flowers' (I, 258).) When the body of the murdered beautiful female is found, her spirit is freed in a (celebrated and effective) Catholic ritual with appropriate music: 'A choir of heavenly voices chaunted the response in which the whole company joined. The organ in full tone began to play' (II, 249). At this point, the earthly singers are joined by *actual* heavenly choirs – 'a new strain of music, much too seraphic to be mortal' (II, 256).

Such moments do not merely gesture to transcendence, they work to bring audiences and readers into a specifically religious experience. Strikingly, both the proxemics and the structuring of the music in *The Haunted Palace* resemble those of the incantation scene in *Remorse*. The 'staging' of both is reminiscent of antiphonal singing (in which a larger choir is divided into two parts which sing from different places). However, unlike usual antiphony, the musical structure is not that of alternation or response. Instead, one choir sings and the other joins them. In both *The Haunted Palace* and *Remorse* there is a difference in degree between the choirs: in the former, the voices are clerical and lay, in the latter, earthly and divine. This difference in degree, I would argue, added to the overwhelming power of the *combination* of the choirs, and the fact that they are heard at different distances (one inside, one outside) acts as a cue. Both the novel and the play use these strategies of accumulation, parallelism and imitation, which conjure up multiple and synchronous acts of worship, to gesture to the breadth of the worshipping universe and bring audience or readers into the act of worship. Notably, *Remorse*'s set included an illuminated chapel, from which the strains are heard, though the interior can't be seen. This figure is also encountered in *The Haunted Palace*, *The Monk* and other Gothic novels of the period. These inaccessible chapels function as the occluded holy of holies, the tabernacle. In *Remorse*, its presence converts the auditorium temporarily into a site of Christian religious worship.

Accounts of the response to Kelly's music for these plays underline the religious nature of the audience experience. Kelly's description of the audience during the *Remorse*'s Invocation is suggestive of a rapt congregation: he writes of a 'great mass of congregated humanity' characterised by its 'undivided attention' (Audio 18). The Jommelli too was destined to contribute to communal worship (Audio 14). Kelly points out that it later became popular in churches (Kelly 1826: II, 184–85).

Wand'ring Demons

The music discussed so far in this section is very 1790s in conception. This is not surprising. *The Castle Spectre* appeared in 1797 and *Remorse*, although it eventually appeared in 1813, is a rewrite of a play (*Osorio*) that was originally offered to Drury Lane in 1797. *Remorse*, however, contains other music that testifies to its later historical moment. The 'Instrument of Glass or Steel', required to perform impromptu to Alvar's descriptions of 'desart Sands', a tornado, a whirlpool and Arctic waters, is given what is essentially a melodramatic cue (Coleridge 1989: 35). Moreover, following the sublime mild spell (Audio 18), there is a (feigned) 'blacker Charm', which is unlike anything heard in this work so far (35) (Audio 20). An example of choral *tempesta*, it is a chromatically varied and noisy number that ends, after moodily stomping around on the tonic for four bars, with a prolonged unresolved diminished seventh – the signature chord of melodrama. This is music horridified that sets out to scare and to curdle the blood.

Audio 20 Michael Kelly, 'Wand'ring Demons hear the spell' from Samuel Taylor Coleridge's *Remorse* (1813). Sung by Issy Bridgeman, Helena Cooke, Guy Cutting and Laurence Williams, accompanied by Seb Gillot. This audio is licensed under a CC BY-NC-ND 4.0 licence. Audio file is also available at www.cambridge.org/McEvoy

---

6 A 'Change of Strain': Melodrama and the Advent of Gothic Music

In the 1790s, the music of the Gothic drama, for the most part, is associated with the world of romance. It is predominantly sung by psychologically healthy people as they celebrate the world of the pastoral, the pleasures of hunting, labour, divine worship and love. Villains tend neither to sing nor to be associated with music. The notable exceptions to the rule are the banditti, but even their numbers tend to be celebratory rather than sinister. They sing of the joys of liberty, the pleasures of drink, or in the case of Le Sage in *The Adopted Child*, of the rural sublime. Music provides a respite from the frenzy and tumult of Gothic villainy, sometimes reaching for the sublime, even in a play like *The Castle Spectre*. The predominant musical idioms of 1790s Gothic drama are not those we associate with a 'Gothic' sound. The very ghost music is serene. This mode of conceiving the music in Gothic continues beyond the 1790s, most notably in operatic romances. Ultimately, however, it was to be supplanted – by a new kind music for the Gothic, one that specialises in the enjoyable commodification of terror.

A Tale of Mystery

Thomas Holcroft's *A Tale of Mystery* (1802) based on René-Charles Guilbert de Pixérécourt's *Coelina* (1801), with music by Thomas Busby, is the first example of a melodrama on the London commercial stage (Figure 18 and Figure 19). Melodrama was an aesthetic experiment, a new genre, in which instrumental music was combined with impassioned verbal utterance and gesture. The *melos* (or melodramatic music) was intended, in the words of Busby, to 'elucidate the action, and heighten the passion of the piece' (Busby 1806: Unpaginated). Although, Busby writes that the 'first essay in this kind of composition was successfully made in Paris soon after the late revolution' (unpaginated), the roots of melodrama, go back further. The form was pioneered by Jean-Jacques Rousseau, whose *Pygmalion*, with music by Horace Coignet, was first produced in 1770. More significant for the development of the English melodrama than Rousseau's rather static work, however,

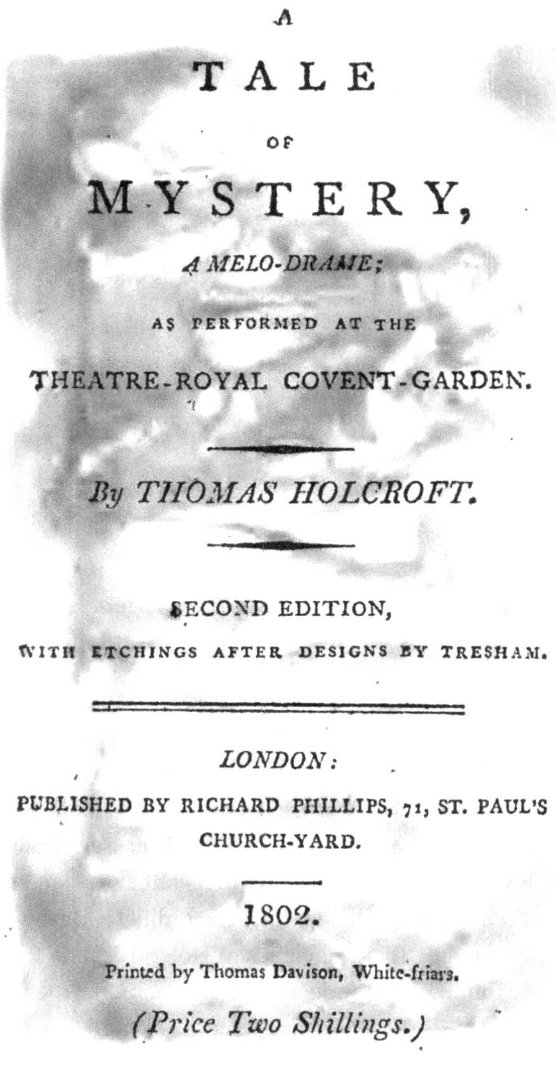

A

TALE

OF

MYSTERY,

A MELO-DRAME;

AS PERFORMED AT THE

THEATRE-ROYAL COVENT-GARDEN.

By *THOMAS HOLCROFT.*

SECOND EDITION,

WITH ETCHINGS AFTER DESIGNS BY TRESHAM.

LONDON:

PUBLISHED BY RICHARD PHILLIPS, 71, ST. PAUL'S
CHURCH-YARD.

1802.

Printed by Thomas Davison, White-friars.

(Price Two Shillings.)

Figure 18 Title page of Holcroft's *A Tale of Mystery* (1802).

was Johann Christian Brandes's and Georg Benda's *Ariadne auf Naxos* (1775). In *Ariadne*, the three characters take it in turns to speak of their pain, their confusion, their discoveries and inner conflicts, separately and, for much of the time, unheard by each other, their utterances placed between what Roger Savage has called a 'succession of highly charged orchestral mood-paintings' (Savage 1991: Unpaginated). As Savage writes elsewhere, *Ariadne* 'is in effect a one-act tragic opera in which no one sings yet to which Benda's music is essential for the creation of atmosphere, the painting of psychology and the heightening of emotion' (Savage 1991–92: 5). *Ariadne*, which aimed for and was considered to have achieved the

Tale of Mystery Act I

Figure 19 Frontispiece to Holcroft's *A Tale of Mystery* (1802).

sublime, was performed across Europe and proved highly influential. It was to be followed by 'reform melodramas that', as Austin Glatthorn argues, 'embraced vocal music and localised sublime moments' and ultimately 'pushed melodrama's generic boundaries to the verge of opera and in the process provided instrumental music with the power to express the sublime without the aid of text' (Glatthorn 2019: 233).

English melodrama is a different beast from those discussed earlier. It doesn't aim for high tragedy, its dialogue is more akin to that of a play, and it is closely, though not exclusively, related to the Gothic. Accordingly, Busby's music for *A Tale of Mystery*, responding to the demands of Holcroft's (and Pixérécourt's) content, is both more limited in emotional range and more frenetic than Benda's music for *Ariadne*. Whereas Benda makes selective use of *Sturm and Drang* motifs, Busby's score relentlessly employs the stylistic elements associated with *tempesta* not only in the grand storm scene but in his *melos* more generally (Figure 20 and Figure 21).

Busby's score was immediately recognised as innovative. A *Times review* notes that the 'hurry and the perturbation of the scene were forcibly depicted by the agitated notes of the orchestra, and this new adjunct to the interest of the drama was immediately felt by the whole audience' (Watson 1926: 353). Busby's melodramatic music, urgent, forceful and highly effective, could be heard at moments of fear and danger – that is, in the very places where music was not to be found in the Gothic drama of the

Figure 20 From Busby's vocal score for *A Tale of Mystery* (c. 1802).
The Bodleian Libraries, University of Oxford, Harding Mus. D 293, p. 11.

1790s. Calculated to deliver shock, it is full of surprise chords, insistent and big dynamic contrasts. As it was designed for short-scale bursts and interjections, it is highly compressed, much of it in 4- or 2-bar phrases. To modern ears, Busby's music has a recognisably 'Gothic' sound. Here are some characteristic examples of his *melos* for *A Tale of Mystery*.

Fiametta enters 'alarm'd and in a hurry' to an actual 'hurry' – a passage of rapidly descending or ascending notes that efficiently fulfils the demand that *melos* should both paint a picture and affect its audience (Busby 1802: 9) (Audio 21a).

Audio 21a Thomas Busby, melo-dramatic music for the cue 'Enter Fiametta alarm'd, and in a hurry' from Thomas Holcroft's *A Tale of Mystery* (1802). Arranged by Seb Gillot. This audio is licensed under a CC BY-NC-ND 4.0 licence. Audio file is also available at www.cambridge.org/McEvoy

Figure 21 From Busby's vocal score for *A Tale of Mystery* (c. 1802). The Bodleian Libraries, University of Oxford, Harding Mus. D 293, p. 12.

The *melos* for the cue 'Bonamo and Fiametta enter in violent contention', employs hectic chord sequences and an unpredictable succession of angular intervals, in its striving to keep audiences on the edge of their seats and thwart their expectations (10) (Audio 21b).

> **Audio 21b** Thomas Busby, melo-dramatic music for the cue 'Bonamo and Fiametta enter in violent contention' from Thomas Holcroft's *A Tale of Mystery* (1802). Arranged by Seb Gillot. This audio is licensed under a CC BY-NC-ND 4.0 licence. Audio file is also available at www.cambridge.org/McEvoy

Because melodramatic music is required to keep its audiences on tenterhooks, phrases very frequently end on cadences that do not return to the tonic, or home chord. Imperfect cadences, as in the last example, leave the phrase hanging, and are designed to increase the feeling of suspense. A particular favourite for melodrama is the unresolved cadence that ends on the horror-inducing diminished seventh, as here (Audio 21c).

> **Audio 21c** Thomas Busby, melo-dramatic music for the cue 'Fran. The same who stabb'd me among the Rocks' from Thomas Holcroft's *A Tale of Mystery* (1802) (Figure 21). Arranged by Seb Gillot. This audio is licensed under a CC BY-NC-ND 4.0 licence. Audio file is also available at www.cambridge.org/McEvoy

Not all of *A Tale of Mystery*'s music is fast and angular. The music for the cue 'Bonamo being about to examine Francisco, commands him to adhere to the truth', marked 'Maestoso', is short but striking (11) (Audio 21d) (Figure 20). The dramatic augmented 6th chord just before the end underlines the seriousness.

> **Audio 21d** Thomas Busby, melo-dramatic music for the cue 'Bonamo being about to examine Francisco, commands him to adhere to the truth' from Thomas Holcroft's *A Tale of Mystery* (1802) (Figure 20). Arranged by Seb Gillot. This audio is licensed under a CC BY-NC-ND 4.0 licence. Audio file is also available at www.cambridge.org/McEvoy

The following sequence from *A Tale of Mystery* illustrates the cumulative affect of the 'in-yer-face' techniques of Busby's music, and the narrative tempo and rhythm of the early melodrama. It is full of rapid, rhythmical insistence, sustained violent contrasts, broken chords and extensive chromaticism. In this passage, Francisco, a mute, who communicates by means of a written board, is being questioned about his background.

> **Audio 21e** Thomas Busby, melo-dramatic music for the cue 'Bonamo being about to examine Francisco, commands him to adhere to the truth' from Thomas Holcroft's *A Tale of Mystery* (1802) (Figure 20). Arranged by Seb Gillot. This audio is licensed under a CC BY-NC-ND 4.0 licence. Audio file is also available at www.cambridge.org/McEvoy

Audio 21f Thomas Busby, melo-dramatic music for the cue 'Francisco with dignity points to Heaven and his Heart' from Thomas Holcroft's *A Tale of Mystery* (1802) (Figure 20). Arranged by Seb Gillot. This audio is licensed under a CC BY-NC-ND 4.0 licence. Audio file is also available at www.cambridge.org/McEvoy

Audio 21g Thomas Busby, melo-dramatic music for the cue 'Bonamo to Francisco, "your Family?"' from Thomas Holcroft's *A Tale of Mystery* (1802) (Figure 20). Arranged by Seb Gillot. This audio is licensed under a CC BY-NC-ND 4.0 licence. Audio file is also available at www.cambridge.org/McEvoy

Audio 21h Thomas Busby, melo-dramatic music for the cue 'Francisco in sorrow gives signs of "forbear", and writes "I must not be known"' from Thomas Holcroft's *A Tale of Mystery* (1802) (Figure 20). Arranged by Seb Gillot. This audio is licensed under a CC BY-NC-ND 4.0 licence. Audio file is also available at www.cambridge.org/McEvoy

Audio 21i Thomas Busby, melo-dramatic music for the cue 'Bon. "why?"' from Thomas Holcroft's *A Tale of Mystery* (1802) (Figure 21). Arranged by Seb Gillot. This audio is licensed under a CC BY-NC-ND 4.0 licence. Audio file is also available at www.cambridge.org/McEvoy

Audio 21j Thomas Busby, melo-dramatic music for the cue 'Francisco. "It is disgraced"' from Thomas Holcroft's *A Tale of Mystery* (1802) (Figure 21). Arranged by Seb Gillot. This audio is licensed under a CC BY-NC-ND 4.0 licence. Audio file is also available at www.cambridge.org/McEvoy

Audio 21k Thomas Busby, melo-dramatic music for the cue 'Bon. "By you?" Fran. gesticulates with agitation' from Thomas Holcroft's *A Tale of Mystery* (1802) (Figure 21). Arranged by Seb Gillot. This audio is licensed under a CC BY-NC-ND 4.0 licence. Audio file is also available at www.cambridge.org/McEvoy

Audio 21l Thomas Busby, melo-dramatic music for the cue 'Franciso being asked who made him dumb, gives signs of horrible recollection' from Thomas Holcroft's *A Tale of Mystery* (1802) (Figure 21). Arranged by Seb Gillot. This audio is licensed under a CC BY-NC-ND 4.0 licence. Audio file is also available at www.cambridge.org/McEvoy

Audio 21m Thomas Busby, melo-dramatic music for the cue 'Fran. The same who stabb'd me among the Rocks' from Thomas Holcroft's *A Tale of Mystery* (1802) (Figure 21). Arranged by Seb Gillot. This audio is licensed under a CC BY-NC-ND 4.0 licence. Audio file is also available at www.cambridge.org/McEvoy

Audio 21n Thomas Busby, melo-dramatic music for the cue 'Bon. "Name them"' from Thomas Holcroft's *A Tale of Mystery* (1802) (Figure 21). Arranged by Seb Gillot. This audio is licensed under a CC BY-NC-ND 4.0 licence. Audio file is also available at www.cambridge.org/McEvoy

Audio 21o Thomas Busby, melo-dramatic music for the cue 'Fran. "Never"' from Thomas Holcroft's *A Tale of Mystery* (1802) (Figure 21). Arranged by Seb Gillot. This audio is licensed under a CC BY-NC-ND 4.0 licence. Audio file is also available at www.cambridge.org/McEvoy

Audio 21p Thomas Busby, melo-dramatic music for the cue 'Bon. "Are they rich?"' from Thomas Holcroft's *A Tale of Mystery* (1802) (Figure 21). Arranged by Seb Gillot. This audio is licensed under a CC BY-NC-ND 4.0 licence. Audio file is also available at www.cambridge.org/McEvoy

Audio 21q Thomas Busby, melo-dramatic music for the cue 'Bon. "Tell me all or quit my house"' from Thomas Holcroft's *A Tale of Mystery* (1802) (Figure 21). Arranged by Seb Gillot. This audio is licensed under a CC BY-NC-ND 4.0 licence. Audio file is also available at www.cambridge.org/McEvoy

Audio 21r Thomas Busby, melo-dramatic music for the cue 'Romaldi being announced, Francisco starts up, struck with alarm' from Thomas Holcroft's *A Tale of Mystery* (1802) (Figure 21). Arranged by Seb Gillot. This audio is licensed under a CC BY-NC-ND 4.0 licence. Audio file is also available at www.cambridge.org/McEvoy

A Tale of Mystery was not only a massive success, but it also sparked a long-lasting fashion for melodrama on the London stage. Its potent blend of action and episodic music impressively fulfilled the conditions of what could be said to be Gothic's mission statement – to provide sensations of pleasurable fear; to keep readers and audiences in suspense; to surprise them; to make them shudder; to keep them begging for more.

The Captive and *Ella Rosenberg*

Matthew Lewis was in the vanguard of writers who took to the melodrama. A mere four months after the opening of *A Tale of Mystery*, he was collaborating with Busby (who had, the previous year, contributed a song to Lewis's, *Alfonso, King of Castile* (1801)). The result was *The Captive*, a monodrama (that is, a melodrama with one speaking actor, as is Rousseau's *Pygmalion*) that premiered at Covent Garden in March 1803. *The Captive* has more in common with *Ariadne auf Naxos* than *A Tale of Mystery*. The resemblance perhaps indicates that Lewis had come across melodrama when in Germany; he might even have attended one of the performances of *Ariadne* directed by Goethe in Weimar in the 1790s. Unlike *A Tale of Mystery*, the cast of *The Captive* is small, the scene deliberately limited, and there is no singing or dancing. As in *Ariadne*, there is a highly distressed woman at the very centre of the action. The protagonist has been imprisoned by a tyrannical husband in a private madhouse and is guarded by a hard-hearted gaoler. Desperately she attempts to cling to her sanity but sees a daemon whose 'eyeballs glare!' and who 'whirls a scorpion high in air!' (Baron-Wilson 1839: I, 240). At the work's climax, she gives 'a loud shriek', cries 'I'm mad! I'm mad!', and 'dashes herself in frenzy upon the ground' (I, 240). Cues for the *melos* include 'Harsh music', 'Music expressing the light growing fainter', and 'the music, changing, expresses that some tender, melancholy reflection has passed her mind' (I, 237, 238). *The Captive* proved too affecting. According to Baron-Wilson, it 'threw a portion of the audience – whose nerves were unable to withstand the dreadful truth of the language and the scene – into hysterics, and the whole theatre into confusion and horror' (I, 233). It was pulled after its first performance. Significantly the next collaboration between Busby and Lewis, *Rugantino* (1805), though a melodrama, was not in Gothic mode.

Busby's music for *The Captive* doesn't seem to have survived. However, its lyrics were set by the composer and soprano Harriet Abrams, who collaborated with Lewis on several occasions (and with him created her most famous song 'Crazy Jane') (Figure 2). 'The Gaoler' is a song of tenderness, innocence and turbulence (Audio 22). In form, it is a seemingly simple strophic song, the likes of which might have appeared in a Gothic drama of the 1790s. However, the speaker's turmoil is captured not only in the changes of her subject position, but also in the sudden surges and falls in volume, the contrasts between the different length phrases, and the bizarrely modern dominant chord over the tonic pedal in the tenth bar.

Audio 22 Harriet Abrams, 'The Gaoler' (1803), lyrics by Matthew Lewis. Sung by Issy Bridgeman, accompanied by Seb Gillot. This audio is licensed under a CC BY-NC-ND 4.0 licence. Audio file is also available at www.cambridge.org/McEvoy

Despite *The Captive*'s lack of success on the stage, melodrama, as Michael Pisani comments, 'with its national heroes, class and ethnic conflicts, sensational scenic effects, and tuneful musical accompaniments, spread like wildfire, not just to the minor theatres of London but also to the regional and provincial theatres of Great Britain and Ireland as well as to theatres in the east-coast cities of the United States' (Pisani 2014: 73). By 1818, as Matthew Buckley notes, when 'the Olympic, Adelphi, Regency, and Coburg all enter the fray … the volume of melodramatic drama in London rose immediately to about five dozen productions per year' (Buckley 2018: 24). Melodrama evolved rapidly, responding to, as well as driving, changes in public taste. Buckley charts its development over the first two decades of the century, noting that Gothic melodrama is overtaken by '"grand romantic" melodrama' set in 'exotic climes', then (after 1810), 'military melodrama' and 'national-historical melodrama', and finally 'domestic melodrama' (18, 20, 21).

Ella Rosenberg, 'a melo-drama in two acts' with Harriet Siddons as the heroic lead, first performed at Drury Lane in 1807, is both, as Buckley notes, a precursor of the domestic melodrama (Buckley 2018: 21) and an example, as Pisani points out, of the 'historical costume dramas with ample opportunities for fight scenes and heroic rescues' (Pisani 2014: 68). It proved extremely popular. Pisani finds evidence that both play text and music were being published 'as late as 1882' (63). Significantly, the *Monthly Review* attributed the attractions of the play to Matthew Peter King's music and the 'decorations of the theatre' rather than to James Kenney's 'flat and insipid' script (Pisani 2014: 66).

King's score shows a sense of heightened confidence in the powers of instrumental music. Whereas Busby had merely supplied a short, pretty 24-bar piece in Bb to introduce *Mystery*'s second act, King provides an atmospheric two-part overture for *Ella*'s (Audio 23). It starts in a gloomy C minor, contains echo effects and sudden forte semi-quavers. A lighter passage in C major precedes the first glimpse of what the published text gives as: 'SCENE. A Rocky Mountaneous [*sic*] Country. Night' (King 1807: 26). NB In King's manuscript, it is scored for strings, horns, oboes, flutes and bassoons. Drums join from the 7th bar of the curtain rise, till the end of the piece when Ella's husband appears (King undated: 71–9).

Audio 23 Matthew Peter King, 'Overture to 2d Act. The Curtain Rises' from James Kenney's melo-drama *Ella Rosenberg* (1807). Arranged by Seb Gillot. This audio is licensed under a CC BY-NC-ND 4.0 licence. Audio file is also available at www.cambridge.org/McEvoy

---

Ella has music for pursuits, disappearances, reappearances, for the opening of a door and the showing of a painting, for changes of states, entries and exits, and after lines such as Storm's 'Ah! ruffians, in my house – Stand Off!' and the villain, Mountfort's 'This is too much! – You forget that insulted love becomes resentment. – Within there!' (Kenney 1807: 12, 11). As well as such frenetic moments, there are those more solemn. In the second act, Ella's protector, the noble Storm, is led away to execution, to the sounds of a dead march, written for clarinets and bassoons and muffled drums. The following music is of the more frenetic and conflicted kind (Audio 24). Ella, having realised that Storm is to be killed and having unsuccessfully sued for mercy, 'Falls to the ground in dispair' [*sic*] at the end of the scene (King 1807: 28). King employs sudden changes in volume and creates momentum with alternating syncopation and sudden silences. NB In King's manuscript, the first section is played by horns, strings and the trombone (an instrument traditionally associated with the dismal). Oboes and flutes join them for the beginning of Ella's agitation. In the middle section, with its inexorable step descent, most of the parts are written with a pathetic flutter upwards, with the exception of the basses and trombone which go resolutely downwards. This 'symphony' could be repeated for as long as needed.

Audio 24 Matthew Peter King, Music for the cue 'Ella Falls to the ground in dispair' (sic) from James Kenney's melo-drama *Ella Rosenberg* (1807). Arranged by Seb Gillot. This audio is licensed under a CC BY-NC-ND 4.0 licence. Audio file is also available at www.cambridge.org/McEvoy

---

Exploding Bridges

Critics have tended to stress the continuities between the Gothic drama and the melodrama. Buckley, for example, refers to *The Castle Spectre* as 'proto-melodramatic' (Buckley 2018: 16), and Gamer writes of 'melodrama's roots in English theatre, particularly the Gothic drama of the 1790s' (Gamer 2018: 31). Pisani too notes that the 'distinctively British form of melodrama also owed a great deal of its unique atmosphere to the late eighteenth-century surge in gothic literature and gothic drama' (Pisani 2014: 54). These points are all valid. As regards the specifically dramatic aspects of the two there is a great deal of crossover between, for example, *The Castle Spectre* and *A Tale of Mystery*. However, in relation to the *melos*, there are significant differences between the drama of the 1790s and the melodrama. The tendency of the music of 1790s Gothic drama is to provide a respite from the scary elements of the plot. Busby's melodramatic music, on the contrary, is meant to underline them. It is designed to – and did – provoke feelings of shock, suspense, alarm and unease in the audience.

Melodramatic music differs from the music of earlier Gothic drama not merely because of its new style with its 'Gothic'-sounding musical idioms, but also because of the *way* it treats music. Supposed to point up and accompany the action, to enunciate that which characters cannot speak and to set scenes, it is not conceived of as emanating from *within* the world of the drama, but rather comes from *outside* it. In the pre-Busby works we've looked at, music is primarily diegetic. (*The Castle Spectre*'s music for the ghost's appearance is the exception to the rule (Audio 14) (Figure 15 and Figure 16).) Apart from the instrumental accompaniment, the music is produced by the characters on stage (or characters who are part of the action but are off stage) and heard by them. Melodramatic music, by contrast, isn't supposed to be produced *within* the world of the play. It works directly on the audience, suggesting and engendering the appropriate affects. It is non-diegetic. Rather than being heard by the characters on stage it is heard by the audience. Melodramatic music is the ancestor of *our* Gothic music, the kind that, to quote Isabella van Elferen writing about the soundtracks of horror films, 'seems to emanate from nowhere, a phantom sound generated by a disembodied presence', a 'sonic imp [which] enters perception through the back door and there performs its destabilising work' (Elferen 2012: 4, 5).

Melodrama changed tastes and created new expectations about what music could do, how it could sound, where it could feature and how it might function within the world of the play. Music no longer had to have an explanation within the action of the play for its presence. It was justification enough that it accompanied the action and worked on its audiences. Increasingly, dramatic productions of all genres, even operatic romances, make use of melodramatic music. *The Devil's Bridge* (1812), for example, features 'Wild music' at the nail-biting climax in which Belino appears on a bridge which is due to explode. Significantly, however, the melodramatic music is not included in the handsome and otherwise full vocal score.

The trajectory of Michael Kelly's career provides an interesting way of thinking through some of the larger changes that were taking place in the period. Kelly was, above all, a vocalist whose forte was melody rather than harmony. In his *Reminiscences*, he writes that Mozart attempted to dissuade him from wasting his efforts on the 'dry' 'study of counterpoint', saying, 'Nature has made you a melodist' and 'Melody is the essence of music' (Kelly 1826: I, 227–28). Kelly's compositions *are* melodic. They play to the strengths of the voice. He tends to leave large instrumental numbers to other composers. As long as music was required to relate to the melodic world of romance, Kelly was the composer to approach. His compositions for *Adelmorn the Outlaw* are described by Baron-Wilson as 'sweet and appropriate' (Baron-Wilson 1839: I, 221). After the melodrama takes hold, his music for Gothic productions doesn't cut the mustard. This can be most clearly seen in his score for Lewis's *The Wood Daemon* (1807). There are some simple dances, marches and grand marches, and some lovely vocal numbers. Despite nice touches for some of the melodramatic cues (threes against twos and fours, a couple of sultry G flats, and some staccato tick-tocks as the characters race against the giant clock that dominates the stage), his music is underpowered.

When Lewis revised *The Wood Daemon*, he got Matthew Peter King on board, to transform it from what Kelly called a 'Grand Dramatic Romance' to a 'Grand Romantic Opera'. It appeared in 1811, with even greater success, as *One O'Clock*. The earlier version had started with Kelly's hunting music and an invocation to the spirits. *One O'Clock*, by contrast, is introduced by an overture laden with the figures associated with melodramatic music (Audio 25). It is an unashamed succession of diminished seventh and augmented sixth chords, short phrases that abruptly end, sudden sforzandos, insistent repetition, violent contrasts in volume, continual refusal to return to the tonic and disturbing tremolando thrown in for good measure.

Audio 25 Matthew Peter King, opening of the overture to Matthew Lewis's *One O'Clock or The Knight and the Wood Daemon* (1811). Arranged by Seb Gillot. This audio is licensed under a CC BY-NC-ND 4.0 licence. Audio file is also available at www.cambridge.org/McEvoy

---

Very broadly speaking, between the 1790s and the 1820s, there is a turn in the Gothic drama from music that is primarily melodic, vocal and diegetic, towards music that is instrumental and non-diegetic and specialises in disturbing harmonies and textures. The music of the earlier period is associated with romance and the promise of escape. As Boaden writes, discussing Storace's music for *The Haunted Tower*, '[t]he composers of that time cultivated a pure and flowing melody like Paesiello [*sic*]; it could be 'heard with unabated delight' (Boaden 1825: II, 13). By contrast, the music for the next generation of Gothic drama underscored Gothic affects associated with shock and suspense and was capable of inducing thrills even without narrative reinforcement. It was to become *the* music of Gothic.

'Wild and Discordant Notes'

Melodrama saw the development of what Pisani calls 'a common musical practice, within which ambitious actors, managers, and orchestra leaders often strove to make the form more dramatically compelling' (Pisani 2018: 110). Its assemblage of musical techniques came to be identified as the sound of the

Gothic. Not only was its musical language highly affective, but the way it was deployed was eminently suggestive. Heard by the audience, but unheard by the characters on stage, it served to make the latter seem more vulnerable and the former feel more divorced from the communal reality of the play. It made the theatre potentially a place of atomised scare for the audience, and engendered a sense that those onstage, unaware of the cues that signal the nature of the world around them, are characterised by a profound uncomprehending naivety.

The rise of melodrama succeeded not merely in transforming the music of the stage, but also in effecting a change in the significance of music in Gothic prose fiction. After 1802, its influence can be seen in novels which focus on strange new kinds of music and feature new musical scenarios. Charlotte Dacre's *Zofloya*, like Lewis's *The Monk*, has supernatural music. The arrival of Zofloya is accompanied by the 'sweetest sounds' of an exotic instrument: 'the tremulous vibration of a double-toned flute, sounding as it were from a distance' (Dacre 1997: 177–78). However, Dacre presents the music in a manner subtly different from Lewis's. She is more interested in auditor than performer, in affect rather than effect. The reactions of her anti-heroine, fast-changing and violently contrasting, are akin to the responses of audiences of melodrama. The 'lovely melody by turns softened and agitated her . . . Still the soft tones continued, and kept her on the rack between pain and pleasure' (178). Victoria is a 'resistless' listener, whose 'turbulent emotions' come and go until the music stops (178). First, she is swayed to 'love' and 'impetuous passion', then a 'melancholy cadence suggested to her sickening soul, that him so franticly adored might never be hers'. (178). The scene-setting also suggests melodrama. The 'idolized form of Henriquez, in all the grace of his youthful beauty', which the 'soft tones . . . brought before her [Victoria's] view', is reminiscent of a melodramatic tableau (178). Later, Victoria is stirred by music that, like melodramatic music, comes from a source not pictured on stage, as it were; it is produced by 'the magical powers of' an 'invisible musician' (213).

The anonymous *The Ruins of Selinunti* (1813) has a flageolet played in the hectic style reminiscent of melodramatic music. 'In this dulcet tumult he continued, till the late bold swell sunk to mild piano, and then fled like the wild and incoherent strains of Eolus, wandering uncontrouled o'er his melancholic harp' (Anonymous 1813: II, 11). Later in the book, a thrilling escapade is highly suggestive of the rhythms of melodrama, with fragmented snatches of melody, an agitated listener and a frenetic to-and-fro-ing between music and action. Don Seggio recounts that in a 'spicy grove, the sounds of plaintive music swam on the atmosphere' and 'accordant feelings urged me to seek a proximity to the harmony' (II, 220). As soon as he leaves the grove, the notes stop and he experiences confused and agitated reactions very like those of the audience of a melodrama. Another sudden 'change of strain' interrupts his 'whirlpool of conjectures' only for it also to stop abruptly (II, 220). In the sudden quietness, Seggio hears only the 'shrill scream' of a lizard, but as he moves towards a 'strange cottage, the music again commenced with masterly execution' (II, 222, 223). Seggio is left 'in a vortex of astonishment' (II, 223). A few days later, the music at the cottage alerts Seggio to an intended assassination. Again, both the description and the scenario suggest melodrama. The 'invisible musician', whom he can't find anywhere, 'again gave tone to wild and discordant notes'; the sound is 'instantly drowned in a more detonating noise' (II, 227).

Haunted Music Rooms

Early in the nineteenth century, as melodrama's compelling but disturbing sounds take hold, music rooms in novels start to become troubling places. Rather than places of recreation for beleaguered heroines, they are associated with moments of fear and moral and intellectual confusion. In the climactic moments of Mrs. Norris's *Julia of England* (1808) Julia is led by the 'child of nature' Theresa, to a long-forgotten music room (Norris 1808: IV, 48). It contains a half-finished painting 'the colourings on which were faintly discernable [*sic*] through the dust', and 'a music book and a volume of Shakespeare . . . open on the table. "What an odious place!" cried Theresa. "But no wonder: nothing has been touched since the old Marchioness died"' (IV, 75). In Ann Maria Porter's *The Fast of St Magdalen* (1819), when the heroine retreats into a 'retired music-room' a 'confusion of alarming images swam before her disordered sight (Porter 1819: II, 3). The 'trembling horror-struck Therese' in Sarah Green's *The Carthusian Friar* (1814) cries out '"O madame, for Heaven's sake . . . do not enter the music room; it is most assuredly haunted!"' (Green 1814: IV, 43). Such music rooms are not merely places where narratives of identity, family history and crime coalesce, their presentation gestures to the lost musical vision of the 1790s. The interior of the music room in *The Carthusian Friar* is dingy, its doors have 'rusty hinges', instruments are broken, music books are 'covered with dust' (Green 1814: III, 88); it is 'long indeed, since' it has 'been opened' (IV, 43). The assemblage of instruments in *Julia of England* gestures to a new musical hierarchy where different instruments dominate. 'A large organ filled up one end of the apartment; a harp near it was dilapidated of every string' (IV, 75).

'No–No–No–Never–Never More!'

By the 1820s, it is difficult to find a Gothic novel in which music is wholeheartedly associated with the world of romance and transcendence. Some novels, like Mary Shelley's *Frankenstein* (1818) contain little music (though the stage adaptation *Presumption* (1823), an interesting hybrid of opera and melodrama, is full of music). In other novels, music becomes a signifier of Gothic trials and tribulation. In Charles Maturin's *Melmoth the Wanderer* (1820), music has, as it were, fallen. The child of nature, Immalee, sings a 'wild song of desperation and love to the echoes of the advancing storm' (Maturin 1989: 315). A despairing lover, 'sunk on the earth' at dusk, hears music that 'seemed designed to echo the words – 'No–no–no–never–never more!', but rather than being a Radcliffean fusion of feeling, landscape and music, part of some Providential design, these notes are 'played accidentally' (489). In Gothic novels of this period, music is increasingly associated with suspicion, madness and unease. Reflecting the non-diegetic tendency of music in the melodrama, novels frequently feature interiorised music or music that can only be heard by one person. Don Seggio in *Selinunti* is inclined 'to believe' his music-accompanied experience to be 'a delusion' (Anonymous 1813: II, 224). In *Melmoth*, Stanton is considered 'insane' when he hears 'a strain of music, soft, solemn, and delicious,' which 'breathed round him, audibly ascending from the ground, and increasing in sweetness and power till it seemed to fill the whole building' (Maturin 1989: 43). Ironically, he is in a playhouse.

Overwhelmingly, in the later nineteenth century, the music of Gothic literature is Gothic music. Most commonly malign, associated with fear, disorientation, threat and haunting, it is the kind of music which, as Elferen writes, is a 'disruptive hauntographical agent', which 'is always spectral', which 'makes the past return and overlay the present' (Elferen 2012: 29, 4, 5). However, fiction throughout the century compulsively revisits the scenarios of 1790s musical romance, through allusions to stray eighteenth-century airs, to music in the mountains or foreign musicians. In Elizabeth Gaskell's 'The Old Nurse's Story' (1852), a, now seemingly obligatory, 'great organ' is heard 'booming and swelling away in the distance' although 'all broken and destroyed inside' (Cox and Gilbert 2003: 6, 7). In this story, the tropes of Radcliffean musical romance are left to fight it out like dogs in a pit, till each is destroyed: social sympathies, persecuted females and the natural world. The 'foreign musician who made such beautiful music, that they said the very birds on the trees stopped their singing to listen', disappears after fathering a child (13–14). An old music-lover becomes his granddaughter's murderer, turning her (and her mother) out on to the Fells where the former dies of 'the frost and the cold' (15). M R James's story 'Lost Hearts' (1895) achieves some of its most disturbing affects with ingredients strikingly similar to Gaskell's: a vile older man is the murderer of a foreign child associated with music and romance. The child ghost – Giovanni Paoli, a strolling Italian hurdy-gurdy player, murdered in 1805 – is both pathetic and terrifying: 'a thin shape, with black hair and ragged clothing' who 'raised his arms in the air with an appearance of menace and of unappeasable hunger and longing', with a 'black and gaping rent' where his heart has been torn out (James 1960: 33).

In J Meade Falkner's novella *The Lost Stradivarius* (1895), eighteenth-century music, relayed to, and received by, the protagonist in a manner akin to the melodrama, is the sinister vehicle of possession. John Maltravers plays the 'Gagliarda' of the 'Areopagita' suite on his violin only to hear 'behind him a creaking of the wicker chair' (Falkner 1991: 6). Some days later, his accompanist finds that the same music 'possesses a singular power of assisting the imagination to picture or reproduce such scenes as those which it no doubt formerly enlivened' and that his playing of the sixteenth bar is accompanied by 'a sense almost of some catastrophe' (13, 14).

In this later nineteenth-century fiction, Radcliffean musical tropes are summoned to be destroyed. Their deconstruction serves as a handy register of perversity and fallen-ness, signalling to readers the loss of the world of romance, the destruction of innocence and the emptying-out of the Providential mode. The negation of Radcliffe's musical tropes indicates that there is no guarantee of the protagonist's safety and shuts down the possibility of transcendence. However, the complex and holistic Radcliffean mode is never treated as mere naivety. Later Gothic works might stage its ritual murder time and time again, but they look to the Radcliffean romance with a sense of profound sadness and 'unappeasable hunger and longing'. The 'black and gaping rent' that lies where Giovanni Paoli's heart should be, testifies to the loss of the musical vision of the 1790s.

References

Abrams, Harriet, 'The Goaler [sic]' (London: Lavenu & Mitchell, undated).

[Amos, A.], 'Shelley and His Contemporaries at Eton', *The Athenaeum* 1068 (1848): 390–391.

Andrews, Miles Peter, *The Mysteries of the Castle* (Dublin: P. Wogan, 1795).

Anonymous, *Ellen Le Clair* (London: R Harrild, 1810).

Anonymous, *The Ruins of Selinunti* (London: Minerva Press, 1813).

Anonymous, 'Mrs Radcliffe', in *The Annual Biography and Obituary for the Year 1824* (London: Longman, 1824), pp. 89–105.

Anonymous, 'Michael Kelly', in *The Annual Biography and Obituary for the Year* 1827 (London: Longman, 1827), pp. 34–61.

Arnold, Samuel, *The Castle of Andalusia: Originally Published by John Bland, London 1782*, introduction by Robert Hoskins (London: Stainer & Bell, 1991).

The Overture to the Italian Monk (London: no publisher named, 1797).

Attwood, Thomas (c. 1792), *The Prisoner* (London: Longman and Broderip).

The Adopted Child (London: Longman and Broderip, 1795).

Baron-Wilson, Margaret (ed.), *The Life and Correspondence of M. G. Lewis*, 2 Vols (London: Henry Colburn, 1839).

Beattie, James, 'On Poetry and Music, as They Affect the Mind', in *Essays* (Edinburgh: William Creech, 1776), pp. 347–580.

Birch, Samuel, *The Adopted Child* (Dublin: George Folingsby, 1799).

Bishop, Henry R., *The Maniac* (London: Goulding, 1810).

Boaden, James, *The Italian Monk* (London: G. G. & J. Robinson, 1797).

Memoirs of the Life of John Philip Kemble Esq (London: Longman, 1825).

The Plays of James Boaden, edited with an introduction by Steven Cohan (New York: Garland, 1980).

Buckley, Matthew 'Early English Melodrama', in Carolyn Williams (ed.), *The Cambridge Companion to English Melodrama* (Cambridge University Press, 2018), pp. 13–30.

Busby, Thomas (c. 1802), *The Tale of Mystery*, (London: E Riley).

A Complete Dictionary of Music (London: T Phillips, 1806), 2nd ed.

Castle, Terry, 'Chapter 8: The Spectralization of the Other in *The Mysteries of Udolpho*', in *The Female Thermometer: Eighteenth-Century Culture and the Invention of the Uncanny* (New York and Oxford: Oxford University Press, 1995), pp. 101–119.

Chao, Noelle, 'Musical Listening in *The Mysteries of Udolpho*', in Phyllis Weliver and Katharine Ellis (eds.), *Words and Notes in the Long Nineteenth Century* (Woodbridge: The Boydell Press, 2013), pp. 85–101.

Clarke-Whitfield, John, '"Soft as the Silver Ray That Sleeps"' (London: Robert Birchall, 1808).

Cobb, James (c. 1789), *The Haunted Tower* (London: J. Sellers).

Coleridge, Samuel Taylor 'The Voice from the Side of Etna, or, the Mad Monk: An Ode, in Mrs Ratcliff's manner' (2022) http://rictornorton.co.uk/gothic/colerid3.htm. [last accessed 5 May 2023].

    Remorse 1813 (Oxford: Woodstock Books, 1989).

Colman, George, *The Iron Chest* (London: Cadell & Davies, 1796).

Cox, Jeffrey (ed.), *Seven Gothic Dramas, 1789–1825* (Athens: Ohio University Press, 1992).

Cox, Michael and Gilbert, R. A. (eds.), *The Oxford Book of Victorian Ghost Stories* (Oxford: Oxford University Press, 2003).

Cullen, Stephen, *The Haunted Priory* (London: J. Bell, 1794).

Dacre, Charlotte, *Zofloya*, edited by Kim Ian Michasiw (Oxford: Oxford University Press, 1997).

Da Ponte, Lorenzo, *La Cosa Rara* (London: C. Etherington for M. Gallerino, 1789).

Dubois, Pierre, *Music in the Georgian Novel* (Cambridge: Cambridge University Press, 2015).

Elferen, Isabella van, *Gothic Music: The Sounds of the Uncanny* (Cardiff: University of Wales Press, 2012).

Falkner, J. Meade, *The Lost Stradivarius*, edited by Edward Wilson (Oxford: Oxford University Press, 1991).

Farley, Charles, *Raymond and Agnes* (London: T. N. Longman, 1797).

Fenwick, Eliza, *Secresy* (London: Pandora Press, 1989).

Fiske, Roger, *English Theatre Music in the Eighteenth Century* (Oxford: Oxford University Press, 1973).

Foley, Matt, 'Towards an Acoustics of Literary Horror', in Kevin Corstorphine and Laura R. Kremmel (eds.), *The Palgrave Handbook to Horror* (London: Palgrave, 2018), pp. 457–68.

Gamer, Michael, 'Gothic Melodrama' in Carolyn Williams (ed.), *The Cambridge Companion to English Melodrama* (Cambridge: Cambridge University Press, 2018), pp. 31–46.

Garlington, Aubrey S. "Gothic' Literature and Dramatic Music in England, 1781–1802', *Journal of the American Musicological Society* 15:1 (1962): 48–64.

Girdham, Jane, *English Opera in Late Eighteenth-Century London: Stephen Storace at Drury Lane* (Oxford: Oxford University Press, 1997).

Glatthorn, Austin, 'The Legacy of "Ariadne" and the Melodramatic Sublime', *Music and Letters* 100:2 (2019): 233–70. https://doi.org/10.1093/ml/gcy116. [last accessed 4 June 2023].

Green, Sarah, *The Carthusian Friar*, 4 Vols (London: Sherwood, 1814).

Hasworth, H. H. *The Lady of the Cave*, 3 Vols (London: Printed at the Minerva Press for Lane and Newman, 1802).

Hatton, Ann Julia, *Secret Avengers*, 4 Vols (London: Minerva Press, 1815).

Hazlitt, William, *Lectures on the English Poets and the English Comic Writers*, edited by William Carew Hazlitt (London: George Bell, 1899).

A View of the English Stage (London: John Warren, 1821).

Heartwell, Henry, *The Castle of Sorrento* (London: Cadell and Davies, 1799).

Holcroft, Thomas, *A Tale of Mystery* (London: R. Phillips, 1802).

Horn, Charles Edward, and Braham, John (c. 1812), *The Devils Bridge* (London: Goulding).

Isaacs, Mrs F., *Glenmore Abbey*, 3 Vols (London: Printed at the Minerva Press, for Lane, Newman, 1805).

James, M. R., *Ghost Stories of an Antiquary* (Harmondsworth: Penguin, 1960).

Kelly, Michael, *The Castle Spectre* (London: J Dale, 1798).

'Cross My Hand & You Shall Know' (London: Corri, Dussek, 1799).

(c. 1807), *The Wood Daemon* (London: M. Kelly).

(c. 1813), 'The Invocation in the Popular Tragedy of *Remorse*' (London: Falkner and Christmas).

Reminiscences of Michael Kelly (London: Henry Colburn, 1826) 2nd ed.

Kenney, James, *Ella Rosenberg* (London: Longman, 1807).

King, Matthew Peter (c. 1807), *Ella Rosenberg* MS score, British Library, Add MS 31767.

(c.1807), *Ella Rosenberg* (London: Pearce).

(c. 1811), *One O'Clock* (London: Clementi).

Kokot, Joanna, 'Between Harmony and Chaos: Poetry and Music in Ann Radcliffe's *The Mysteries of Udolpho*', in Jakub Lipski and Jacek Mydla (eds.), *The Enchantress of Words, Sounds and Image: Anniversary Essays on Ann Radcliffe (1764–1823)* (Palo Alto: Academica Press, 2015), pp. 53–70.

Lathom, Francis, *Astonishment!!!*, 2 Vols (London: T. N. Longman and O. Rees, 1802).

Lee, Sophia, *The Recess*, 3 Vols (London: T. Cadell, 1786).

Lewis, Matthew, *The Monk*, edited by Howard Anderson, (Oxford: Oxford University Press, 1995).

The Castle Spectre (London: J. Bell, 1798) 4th ed.

(c.1807), *The Wood Daemon* (London: J. Scales, undated).

One O'Clock (London: Lowndes, 1811).

Lipski, Jakub, 'Ann Radcliffe and the Sister Arts Ideal', in Jakub Lipski and Jacek Mydla (eds.), *The Enchantress of Words, Sounds and Image: Anniversary Essays on Ann Radcliffe (1764–1823)* (Palo Alto: Academica Press, 2015) pp. 3–20.

Maturin, Charles, *Melmoth the Wanderer*, edited by Douglas Grant (Oxford: Oxford University Press, 1989).

Milbank, Alison, 'Ways of Seeing in Ann Radcliffe's Early Fiction', in Dale Townshend and Angela Wright (eds.), *Ann Radcliffe, Romanticism and the Gothic* (Cambridge: Cambridge University Press, 2014), pp. 85–99.

Moody, Jane, *Illegitimate Theatre in London, 1770–1840* (London: Cambridge University Press, 2000).

Nicholson, Mr, MS music for *The Wild Boy of Bohemia*, Theatre Archive, V & A, ref: S.296–1981.

Norris, Mrs, *Julia of England* (London: Samuel Tipper, 1808).

North, Francis, *The Kentish Barons* (London: J. Ridgway, 1791).

Noske, Frits, 'Sound and Sentiment: The Function of Music in the Gothic Novel', *Music & Letters* 62:2 (1981): 162–75.

O'Keeffe, John, *The Castle of Andalusia* ([Dublin]: Sold by the Booksellers, 1783).

Palmer, A. H., *The Life and Letters of Samuel Palmer* (London: Seeley, 1892).

Palomba, Giuseppe, *Gli Schiavi per Amore* (London: D. Stuart, 1787).

Pearce, William, Licenser's copy, *The Nunnery* (c. 1785), LA 696, Larpent Collection, Huntingdon Library.

    Licenser's copy, *The Midnight Wanderers* February 9 1793, LA 971, Larpent Collection, Huntingdon Library.

    The Midnight Wanderers (Dublin: P. Byrne, 1793).

    Licenser's copy, *Netley Abbey* March 26 1794, LA1016, Larpent Collection, Huntingdon Library.

    Netley Abbey (London: T. N. Longman, 1794).

Peck, Louis, *A Life of Matthew G. Lewis* (New Haven: Harvard University Press, 1961).

Pisani, Michael, *Music for the Melodramatic Theatre in Nineteenth-Century London and New York* (Iowa City: University of Iowa Press, 2014).

    'Melodramatic Music', in *The Cambridge Companion to English Melodrama*, edited by Carolyn Williams (Cambridge University Press, 2018), pp. 95–111.

Porter, Anna Maria, *The Fast of St. Magdalen*, 3 Vols (London: Longman, 1819).

Price, Curtis, Milhous, Judith and Hume, Robert D., *Italian Opera in Late Eighteenth-Century London, Volume 1: The King's Theatre, Haymarket, 1778–1791* (Oxford: Clarendon Press, 1995).

Radcliffe, Ann, *The Castles of Athlin and Dunbayne*, edited by Alison Milbank (Oxford: Oxford University Press, 1995).

    A Sicilian Romance, edited by Alison Milbank (Oxford: Oxford University Press, 1993).

    The Romance of the Forest, edited by Chloe Chard (Oxford: Oxford University Press, 1986a).

    The Mysteries of Udolpho, edited by Bonamy Dobrée (Oxford: Oxford University Press, 1986b).

    The Italian, edited by Frederick Garber (Oxford: Oxford University Press, 1986c).

    Gaston de Blondeville with a Memoir of the Author, edited by Thomas Noon Talfourd (London: Henry Colburn, 1826).

Reeve, Clara, *The Old English Baron*, edited by James Trainer (Oxford: Oxford University Press, 2003).

Rose, John, *The Prisoner* (London: C. Lowndes, 1792).

Sadie, Stanley (ed.), *The New Grove Dictionary of Opera*, 4 Vols (Oxford: Oxford University Press, 1997).

Saggini, Francesca, *The Gothic Novel and the Stage: Romantic Appropriations* (Abingdon: Routledge, 2015).

Saglia, Dietro, 'A portion of the Name': Stage Adaptations of Radcliffe's Fiction, 1794–1806', in Dale Townshend and Angela Wright (eds.), *Ann Radcliffe, Romanticism and the Gothic* (Cambridge: Cambridge University Press, 2014), pp. 219–36.

Sanderson, James (c. 1801), 'The Cottage of Peace' (London: E. Riley).

Savage, Roger, 'Melodrama Enlightened', in Orchestra of the Age of Enlightenment London Series booklet (1991–92), pp. 3–6.

    Programme-note for Benda's *Ariadne*, Orchestra of the Age of Enlightenment concert, (London, Winter 1991).

Scott, Walter, 'Mrs Radcliffe' in Austin Dobson (ed.), *Lives of the Novelists* (Oxford: Oxford University Press, 1906), pp. 302–42.

Shaw, Thomas (c. 1789), *The Island of St. Marguerite* (London: S. A. and P. Thompson).

Shelley, Percy Bysshe, *Zastrozzi* and *St Irvyne*, edited by Stephen C. Behrendt (Oxford: Oxford University Press, 1986).

Shield, William, *The Nunnery* (London: Longman, 1785).

    The Midnight Wanderers (London: Longman, 1793).

    Netley Abbey (London: Longman, 1794).

    The Mysteries of the Castle (London: Preston, 1795).

Siddons, Henry, *The Sicilian Romance* (London: J. Barker, 1794).

    A Tale of Terror (London: James Ridgway, 1803).

Sleath, Eleanor, *The Orphan of the Rhine* (London: Folio Press, 1968).

St John, John, *The Island of St Marguerite* (London: J. Debrett, 1789).

Storace, Stephen, *The Haunted Tower* (London: Longman, 1789).

   Mahmoud & the Iron Chest (London: Printed for Mrs. Storace, 1797).

Süner, Ahmet, 'The Sublimating and Suspending Uses of Music in Radcliffe's *the Mysteries of Udolpho*', *Eighteenth-Century Studies* 53:3 (Spring 2020): 447–61.

Townshend, Dale and Wright, Angela (eds.), *Ann Radcliffe, Romanticism and the Gothic* (Cambridge: Cambridge University Press, 2014).

Walpole, Horace, *The Castle of Otranto*, edited by Nick Groom (Oxford: Oxford University Press, 2014).

Watson, Ernest Bradlee, *Sheridan to Robertson: A Study of the Nineteenth-Century London Stage* (Cambridge, MA: Harvard University Press, 1926).

Yorke, R. P. M. *The Haunted Palace*, 3 Volumes (London: Earle and Hemet, 1801).

Acknowledgements

My profound thanks go to Robert Lee who, unpaid, spent many hours on this project, editing and mastering the sound files, editing the film of the lecture-recital, and reading and giving constructive criticism on the written text.

May Lee McEvoy, Rowan Lee McEvoy, David Short and Chris Baldick proved to be indefatigable and generous readers and provided invaluable comments on the manuscript – many thanks to them! Dale Townshend has been a never-tiring source of information and help whose knowledge about Romantic-period Gothic has been essential. Thanks to David Woodcock, so generous with his time and helpful with his advice. Roger Savage proved to be a fount of knowledge about eighteenth- and nineteenth-century opera, and a pleasure to communicate with. I owe him many thanks, both for his answers to my questions and for the questions he posed to me.

Staff at the British Library, the National Library of Ireland, the V&A theatre archives, the Royal College of Music and the Bodleian Libraries, University of Oxford, have been unfailingly helpful. I owe a great debt especially to Jennifer Yellin at the University of Westminster library and Martin Holmes, Alfred Brendel Curator of Music at the Bodleian Libraries, Oxford. They were exceedingly generous in the help they gave me in locating items and finding the best places to search. Equally importantly, Martin helped me to realise when I could stop searching.

My thanks to the British Academy and Leverhulme Trust for the grant that supported my Music of the Gothic project, allowing me to engage the musicians as well as funding trips to archives and the filming of the lecture-recital. Without the grant, this Element simply would not have been possible. Thanks also to the University of Westminster who gave me a semester's sabbatical to work on the Element, paid for various other costs involved in my research and made freely available the University of Westminster Recording Studios where Ollie Dow recorded the tracks swiftly and expertly.

Finally, I thank the musicians who played and sung so brilliantly and movingly and were such a pleasure to work with: Jane Gordon and Sophie Simpson (violins), George White (viola) and Tim Smedley (cello), Richard Lines-Davies (flute and oboe), Alice Lee (clarinet and bassoon), Issy Bridgeman (soprano), Helena Cooke (mezzo-soprano), Guy Cutting (tenor) and Laurence

Williams (bass). Amongst the musicians, my biggest debt of gratitude is to Seb Gillot, who brought so much talent, experience and commitment to the project. Seb assembled the ensemble, conducted, played keyboard and was responsible for the stunning arrangements.

To Rowan, Finn and May

Cambridge Elements ☰

The Gothic

Dale Townshend

Manchester Metropolitan University

Dale Townshend is Professor of Gothic Literature in the Manchester Centre for Gothic Studies, Manchester Metropolitan University.

Angela Wright

University of Sheffield

Angela Wright is Professor of Romantic Literature in the School of English at the University of Sheffield and co-director of its Centre for the History of the Gothic.

Advisory Board

About the Series

Seeking to publish short, research-led yet accessible studies of the foundational 'elements' within Gothic Studies as well as showcasing new and emergent lines of scholarly enquiry, this innovative series brings to a range of specialist and non-specialist readers some of the most exciting developments in recent Gothic scholarship.

Cambridge Elements ≡

The Gothic

Elements in the Series

A full series listing is available at: www.cambridge.org/GOTH